Child of Peace, Lord of Life

Year A, Volume 2

Reflections on the Readings
of the Common Lectionary
(from the Sunday of the Passion
to the Last Sunday after Pentecost)

Herbert O'Driscoll

Anglican Book Centre
Toronto, Canada

1987
Anglican Book Centre
600 Jarvis Street
Toronto, Ontario
Canada M4Y 2J6

Copyright © 1987 by Anglican Book Centre

All rights reserved. No part of this book may be reproduced, stored in a retrieval system, or transmitted, in any form or by any means, electronic, mechanical photocopying, recording, or otherwise, without the written permission of the Anglican Book Centre.

Typesetting by Jay Tee Graphics Ltd.

Canadian Cataloguing in Publication Data

O'Driscoll, Herbert, 1928-
  Child of peace, lord of life: reflections on the readings of the Common Lectionary

ISBN 0-919891-53-5 (v. 1). - ISBN 0-919891-65-9 (v. 2).

1. Bible - Meditations. 2. Bible - Liturgical lessons, English. 3. Bible - Homiletical use. I. Title.

BS511.2.037 1987   220.6   C86-094825-0

for Jim Cruickshank,
fellow priest and friend

Contents

Suggestions for the Use of These Reflections

My intention is that these pages be helpful to anyone who may have the responsibility of giving homilies in the contexts of worship or of leading Bible study based on the Sunday scriptures. They might also be helpful to anyone who wishes to prepare for worship by having some possible applications of scripture suggested for reflection.

At no time do I want to suggest that these reflections are *the* meaning of a particular passage. Most certainly there are particular meanings to every scripture, and it is the task of exegesis to seek those meanings. It is equally true, however, that scripture, like all great literature, is infinitely rich in its capacity to evoke an endless variety of responses in those who come to it. Two thousand years of Christian reflection and three thousand years of Jewish reflection are ample proof of this.

1 Each of these chapters looks at the Old Testament, the Epistle and the Gospel in that order, then the Psalm. I have chosen to do this because very often the Psalm is an expression of themes which may be spread through two or even three of the readings.

2 I think it important to note that each chapter is not structured as a homily. Each reading is taken as significant in itself. Naturally, I have always listened for echoes of one reading in the others, yet my primary goal has been to let each scripture speak with its own integrity. Because of this there will very often be material for homilizing within the treatment of any one reading.

3 Because the full scripture text is readily available to any reader, I have quite often not given the complete sequence of a verse. No such omission is an attempt to manipulate a convenient meaning from scripture.

4 It will be noted that in many cases I have given more space to the first reading. I have done this to encourage the developing recovery of the Old Testament as a source of homily.

5 It may be worth saying a word about the lectionary as having a weekly theme. This is not always immediately evident. Sometimes it simply does not do so. While the compilers of the lectionary have assumed the Gospel to be the primary reading, each of the three readings, because of its being part of an ongoing sequence in its own particular book of the Bible, will sometimes have its own ''word'' for the reader. Certainly, links are always possible, but they are not necessarily ready-made, waiting to be built into a neat three-part homily or meditation or Bible study! However, to the extent that it may be helpful to point out possible patterns and links, I have tried to express an overall theme for each set of readings.

6 These reflections have one purpose. They are not designed to be in themselves merely the material for someone else's preaching or meditation or Bible study. They will have been most richly of use to the extent that they act as a starting point and catalyst for the reader's own reflections.

Acknowledgement

I wish to thank Sue Johnsen for her excellent typing.

Passion (Palm) Sunday

Isaiah 50:4–9a
Philippians 2:5–11
Matthew 27:11–54
Psalm 31:9–16

Theme Throughout these scriptures the experience of Our Lord is paramount. It in turn speaks to us of our experience. His behaviour becomes a possible pattern and grace for ours (Isaiah). His choosing to show power in servanthood calls us to imitate him (Philippians). The terrible questions which echo around his trial echo within us (Matthew).

First Reading

The Lord . . . has given me a tongue . . . to sustain . . . him that is weary

That is true of Our Lord most certainly. From him and from his ministry all of us have been given resources which come as grace to our weariness and our frequent need of help. Likewise each of us can use those resources in the gospels when we are trying to be a means of grace to others in need. The actual words of Our Lord can be immensely healing and sustaining.

The Lord wakens my ear to hear as those who are taught

This can be a word to us about our own potential ministry. In today's society we are discovering the healing power of listening. There can be a ministry of listening and there can be some basic training for it, increasing our sensitivity and our ability to hear what someone may be saying behind the words we are hearing. This ministry does not have to be left to professionals ("those who are taught").

> *I gave my back to the smiters . . . hid*
> *not my face from shame and spitting. . .*
> *I know that I shall not be put to shame*

The images which come immediately to mind are the responses of Our Lord to the events to come later this week. But how can this scripture be a pattern for our own responses in certain circumstances? Where in our lives can there be "smiters, shame, spitting"? All are images of the extremely painful episodes of life. In professional life there can be the unprovoked attack for many reasons and from many directions. The destructive campaign of business rivalry, the seamy struggles of office politics, the take-over attempt, the strike. In personal life the agonized mutual recriminations of divorce, the hurts and betrayals involving the distribution of an estate within a family. The list is long. How do we conduct ourselves with integrity? To retaliate with similar behaviour would be to "confound" the situation, to be "put to shame." If we do find ourselves in such situations, we are asked as a Christian to do at least two things:

> *Behold the Lord God helps me. Who will*
> *declare me guilty?*

First, I realize I am not alone in the situation. I have a living Lord with whom I can share it. I can ask for grace in showing restraint in my actions (one of the fruits of the Holy Spirit is self-control). Secondly, I can examine my own motivations in total honesty before God in confession. I can thus genuinely pray to be shown if I myself am wrong in my attitudes.

Who is my adversary?

A very important question. Are there justifications for his or her stance? Can I respond to them? Is my adversary perhaps not entirely outside me in another but also within me, part of my own self?

Second Reading   *Have this mind among yourselves, which is yours in Christ Jesus*

We have just been asking how one can "have the mind of Christ" in the really painful, vulnerable episodes of life. Here we are given more insights into Christian character.

Not count equality with God a thing to be grasped

Our motivations, our needs, our view of a situation, our objectives are not ultimate values. Nothing in any situation is "god" except God!

Emptied himself, taking the form of a servant

The majesty of Our Lord is his acceptance of servanthood. It is the paradox at the heart of Christian life. It is also the most difficult thing to practice!

He humbled himself and became obedient to death

It is most difficult to empty oneself of status, rights, claims, because to do so involves some dying within ourselves.

Therefore God has highly exalted him

But to accept servanthood, surrender status, do some inner dying is to discover within oneself a new freedom, a new sense of integrity. All of which we see in the pattern of Our Lord's behaviour and the consequences of triumph and resurrection.

Third Reading

Because this passage is so integral to our faith, it is incalculably rich in homily possibilities. For our purposes now I will take four great questions asked in it — three asked by Pilate, one by Jesus — using them for this year's reflection.

Are you the king?

It is Pilate's question in a particular context and linked to a particular people. But it is my question to myself as a Christian. I ask it of myself as I reflect on Jesus Christ. Is he really king in my life? What would that mean if it were so? How do I set about making him so?

Jesus said, ''You have said so''

There is a hint from Our Lord that I who seek him am the only one who can say he is king. He cannot say it for me. He is a king who does not take authority by power. He accepts my allegiance if it is freely given.

Who do you want me to release for you, Barabbas or Jesus?

Pilate's question, echoing in history, is also a question within each of us. There are many levels of my being which demand release from time to time. Barabbas, rattling the doors of his cell, can within me be what Jung called the "shadow" in everyone, the dark side of the self, its demands, its self-centred drives. As I read this word of scripture, I am also being told that I must constantly make choices about what is to be released from within me. I am responsible for those choices.

What shall I do with Jesus who is called Christ?

My choices are many. I can ignore him, difficult though that is. I can regard him as an interesting historical figure. I can use him as the subject of theological study. I can sentimentalize him as a great deal of popular culture does. I can grasp on to him as a source of private grace and at the same time fail to see that he makes demands on my society and its political decisions. On the contrary, I can see him as a romantic revolutionary leader without ever acknowledging that I am called to worship him at his altar and to study his words. There is no end to what I may do with Jesus who is called Christ.

Jesus cried, "My God, my God, why have you forsaken me?"

If any sentence in the gospels resounds with utter reality, it is this. If anything is needed to communicate the utter humanity of Our Lord and the awful cost of that humanity, we possess it here. There is no loneliness, no pain, no depression, no suffering beyond the reach of this cry. From this moment Jesus is beside every human sufferer, offering himself as a companion of grace to our terrible need.

Psalm

Almost every level of human mental agony is in these verses. Depression affects the whole physical being (vv 9, 10). It isolates and thus cuts off the possibility of relationships (v 11). It creates a sense of utter uselessness (v 12) and brings on a feeling of paranoia (v 13). Yet preserved somehow beneath all this is the shining jewel of trust in God (vv 14–16).

Easter — During the Day

Acts 10:34–43
Colossians 3:1–4
John 20:1–18
Psalm 118:14–24

Theme The mighty resurrection of God's Son. The old order overcome. All things made new (Collect). All is very much rooted in reality. The great event comes in a single human life and is to be witnessed to by other ordinary lives (Acts). To believe in Christ risen is to have a reference point beyond history's limits (Colossians). Seeking what is alive and creative in a world of possible death and annihilation is, for a Christian today, to seek where Christ has risen (John).

First Reading   *God shows no partiality . . . in every nation anyone who . . . does what is right is acceptable to him*

Peter, who says these words, has just had his horizons rolled back! A Roman in Caesarea (that most Roman and secular of cities), has obviously had a genuine experience of God! This can only mean that the sphere of God's activity is limitless, certainly infinitely wider than Peter has ever imagined it. But who is "Peter" and where for us is "Caesarea"? Peter is today's Christian and Caesarea is the world of our time. In that world God is calling us to discover his work and creativity in places where we can barely imagine him to be. In what ways can lasers be the light of God, microbiology a formerly hidden part of his glory, space probes an invitation to his creation?

Jesus Christ [he is Lord of all]

In what sense can this be? How can my being a Christian affect the way I think about, experiment with, and use, all the wonders of my time? In the sense that I strive to make him Lord of contemporary experience, as distinct from my Christianity being a tiny religious section of my life cut off from and lost among the great explosion of possibilities in my time.

Beginning from Galilee after the baptism which John preached

Peter is saying that through John the Baptist there is a link back into the long past of the Old Testament events. In just the same way my contemporary Christian faith is linked back through the centuries to those seemingly local, small-stage events of Peter's time. Therefore it is important for me to know exactly what happened! And here we are told,

> *God anointed Jesus with the Holy Spirit*
> *. . . he went about doing good and*
> *healing . . . They put him to death . . .*
> *God raised him . . . he commanded us to*
> *preach . . . everyone who believes in him*
> *receives forgiveness of sins*

Here we have a statement of Christian belief, a kind of early creed. But notice that to Peter the events are not merely external facts, interesting but detached from him. Notice how they affect his life.

> *We are witnesses to all he did . . . God*
> *made him manifest to us who were*
> *chosen as witnesses . . . He commanded*
> *us to testify*

Because of these events Peter is captured by a vocation. A witness is one who not merely sees something but who is prepared to say that he or she saw it. If Christian faith means something to us, then how do we choose to witness to it? This will depend on our personality, but the important thing is that we witness.

> *Witnesses who ate and drank with him*
> *after he rose*

We do this every time we receive the eucharist! The wonder can be lost in familiarity.

> *Everyone who believes in him receives*
> *forgiveness of sins*

Because of Jesus Christ entering the humanity I share, this humanity of mine, with all its faults, is now acceptable to God. My limitations and failures and betrayals, all the shadowed sinful side of me, is known and accepted. I don't have to be a prisoner of guilt. Because Christ came alive, I can "come alive"!

Second Reading *Set your minds on things that are above,*
not on things that are on earth

Some people, it has been said, are so "heavenly" that they are no "earthly" use. Christianity, it has been said, is "pie in the sky when you die." But C.S. Lewis points out that, when we look at the record, a peculiar thing emerges. It is precisely those people whose minds were set on things above who lived most creatively and effectively on earth. In other words, it is those who have a vision beyond what exists who are moved to work in and on what exists. One has only to think of a Wilberforce working for freedom for slaves, a Helder Camara committed to the poor, a Teresa committed to the diseased and dying. It is precisely because these minds are "set on things above" that they possess the steel to withstand the pressure, and sometimes even horror, of a reality to be faced.

> *You have died . . . you also will appear with him in glory*

Is there not a mysterious quality about the kind of people just mentioned? It is as if certain things in them had died — things such as self, fear, ego. In their place a Christ-likeness has appeared in terms of courage, selflessness, peace, resilience.

Third Reading   *Mary Magdalene went to the tomb early, while it was still dark*

In terms of personal experience the image of Mary in the dark hours can have meaning for us. There are times in our lives when we are among "tombs" — in defeat, loss, pain, fear, failure, betrayal. At such times we feel our deepest selves to be in "darkness." We search for the God we knew as companion, as one familiar perhaps in prayer or sacrament, and we find everything to be "empty."

> *She ran and went to Simon Peter and the other disciple*

She sought companionship. She turned to others. So will we as a first step in "darkness" and "emptiness" and the absence of God, if we are wise.

They have taken the Lord . . . we do not know

We, like Mary, confess our loss of faith, our need of help. We realize that "we do not know." We fully acknowledge the darkness of doubt. We do not have to be guilty about loss of belief.

The other disciple saw and believed

One person comes to belief. But he cannot bring belief to Peter or Mary. That must be done by each one individually. Others can help; they can "run" with us in our searching. But each of us makes the decision to say *yes* to the risen Lord.

The disciples went to their homes, but Mary stood weeping outside the tomb

Probably, as we have done to others, they tried to get her away. But sometimes to remain in the presence of whatever agonizes us is not unhealthy. To remain weeping can be healing. Further, it may give us time to begin to examine what we fear, what we have lost, why we are feeling as we are. The angel can, and probably has, come to each of us, asking, "Why are you weeping?"

Because they have taken away my Lord, and I do not know where they have laid him

Mary is looking for Jesus in terms of what she last saw — a limp, lifeless body. So much does she take this for granted that when. . .

She saw Jesus standing, she did not know that it was Jesus

Maybe, just maybe, Jesus and faith in him can die in us because we are looking for the wrong forms and images of him!

Whom do you seek?

So says the risen Christ to us. A past Christ? A figure in history? An intellectualized Christ, interesting for discussion and analysis? A safe, comforting Christ who never disturbs?

Jesus said to her, "Mary"

Read this phrase with your own name. Taste its power. In a sense that is what happened at your baptism. It is what happens again when you renew your baptism.

She turned and said, "Rab-boni!"

What do you and I choose to say to the encounter with Christ? Do we acknowledge him as "Master"?

*Do not hold me . . . go to my brethren
. . . Mary went and said, "I have seen
the Lord"*

Faith cannot be held. It comes and goes. The best way of holding it is, paradoxically, sharing it. Faith is strongest if lived among "brothers and sisters." Notice the utter simplicity of Mary's statement. To witness does not involve complex explanation. For a person to say to another in conversation, naturally and simply, "I have felt the presence of Christ with me in this or that situation," can be very powerful. Nothing else need be said. Even if the subject is changed the simple witnessing can remain and a seed may begin to grow.

Psalm

Joy, hope, liberation, thanksgiving sound in every part of this song. With obvious glee the singer brings out the constant biblical insight that God does the unexpected when least expected! The rejected stone ends up as cornerstone. The carpenter is king! The crucified is alive! God is a God who acts in our lives and in history. Rejoice! Be glad!

Second Sunday of Easter

Acts 2:14a, 22–32
1 Peter 1:3–9
John 20:19–31
Psalm 16:5–11

Theme We hear the voices of the early Christians expressing what the resurrection meant for them. This calls us to decide what it means for us. In both readings, from Acts and Peter's letter, we are left in no doubt that Our Lord's rising meant a whole new way of looking at life. The Gospel passage, as it describes Thomas's experience, is also describing the experience of every one of us in our personal struggle toward faith.

First Reading

Peter, standing with the eleven . . . addressed them

Once there were twelve, then, because of Judas's betraying Jesus, there were only eleven. Now by electing Matthias there are once again twelve. They are twelve as Peter speaks to the crowd. But the mere mention of the word eleven is a reminder that this embryonic church is already wounded. It's far from perfect. It has already known betrayal. In other words, it has learned the unpleasant fact that it is and always will be full of humanity. We do well to realize this when we discover "humanity" in today's community.

> *Jesus, attested with . . . mighty works,*
> *wonders and signs, you crucified*

Notice the seeming paradox which teaches so much. Our Lord has power to effect wonderful things, but this power is not used to protect himself from enmity and violence. In a mysterious way power and a self-chosen vulnerability mingle in Our Lord. It's interesting that this very mixture in our own humanity commends us to one another. We see in one another ''works and wonders and signs'' — great gifts — yet we also realize how vulnerable even the most gifted can be. There is a peculiar irony in the fact that it is often the most gifted who, because of their sensitivity, are most easily ''crucified'' — hurt, pained, wounded.

> *Jesus, delivered up according to the*
> *definite plan and foreknowledge of God*

In saying this Peter is observing something about all our lives. Is there meaning and purpose to the pattern of our lives, the actions we do, the choices we make, the things that happen to us? Peter is not saying that Jesus was a puppet, manipulated by an abitrary God. He is saying that God has created an overall purpose for creation into which the events of Jesus' experience are placed and used. We believe the same to be true of our lives. That is not to say that it is easy to believe this, especially in suffering and sorrow. The alternative is that the pattern of our lives has no meaning, no ultimate purpose.

> *The Lord is at my right hand that I may*
> *not be shaken . . . my heart was great*
> *. . . my flesh will dwell in hope*

This voice of David expresses an attitude about life. It expresses a conviction of God's presence with us. Whether or not this conviction is personally real for oneself, we all know people for whom it is real. To see such faith awes us. We also see that it produces an extraordinary degree of confidence, joy, and hope — the three qualities mentioned in this scripture.

> *Thou hast made known to me the ways of life*

Being convinced of God's presence and love does not give a set of neat answers about life. What it gives is the over-riding knowledge that there is a "way" to live, a "way" to search for meaning when there seems no meaning, a "way" to use trust and faith when explanation fails, a "way" to be capable of "gladness," not because of what life has brought but because there is a sense of God's presence in the particular situation.

> *He [David] spoke of the resurrection of Christ . . . not abandoned to Hades . . . of that we all are witnesses*

It would be easy to let this scripture go by as merely a long-ago piece of allegory, but it can be heard as a call to every Christian. In some sense, each of us must "speak of the resurrection of Christ," whether by our actual speech or our way of life and faith. It may be our expressed conviction that our life is created for a reality beyond the shadowlands of death — not abandoned to Hades. Having such a conviction or hope in my life can give me the grace to witness to Our Lord's risen power.

Second Reading   *Born anew to a living hope through the resurrection of Jesus Christ*

This passage sounds the empowerment which the fact of Our Lord's resurrection had for this first generation of Christians. It means nothing less than the coming to birth in them of an essentially new attitude toward being alive. To what degree is that true in our experience?

> *An inheritance . . . imperishable . . .*
> *unfading . . . kept in heaven*

It is as if the parameters of human life have been rolled back, revealing far greater dimensions than it possessed before. This is what belief in the resurrection does. Time is given the context of eternity; earth is given the context of heaven. The practical application of such an attitude is that it enables a man or woman to "rejoice . . . though [they] may have to suffer various trials" — the events of human experience are given a context greater than themselves. There is a hope beyond them.

Third Reading

Part of the power of scripture lies in the fact that it does not indulge in unreality. Here we have acted out a struggle that goes on in us all. In this sense, everyone's name contains the name of Thomas.

> *Jesus stood among them and said,*
> *"Peace be with you"*

It is easy to miss the fact that this short, vivid scripture expresses the goal of much church life today. The altar among us all, the exchanging of Our Lord's peace — both so-called "changes" or "innovations" in practice — are a modelling of this moment in Our Lord's relationship with his disciples.

> *He showed them his hands and his side*

Our Lord does not pretend that resurrection is without cost. To say that Christian faith can give me the grace to "rise" in the face of the various "deaths" in human experience does not deny that such "risings" can be at great cost. That cost will show in some element of "woundedness" in my life. In some sense, I will not be able to avoid "showing . . . hands and side."

Even so, I send you

The vocation we are sent to is to live life on the basis described above.

When he had said this, he breathed on them

I am not merely sent upon a costly and challenging vocation. I am also given a grace, a spirit, a measure of my Lord's spirit, to enable me to respond.

When Jesus came . . . Thomas was not with them

In Christian experience my Lord comes to me in various ways and at different times. That affects my thoughts, my attitudes, my faith. But there is also a part of me, the "Thomas" part of me, who is not there. This part that stands aloof from faith, questions and rationalizes, and can at times dismiss the shared faith of the worshipping community which in different ways says to me, "We have seen the Lord."

Eight days later Thomas was with them

There are, thank God, moments when all of the many elements of discipleship within me are together and present when my Lord comes, even the "Thomas" part of me! Those moments are unpredictable and varied. They may occur in unexpected places and unexpected times. In such moments I am brought to a reality that is as real as touch.

Put out your hand

It may be worth recalling this scripture whenever we prepare to extend our hands to receive the bread of eucharist. In that moment we can be conscious of putting out our hand and placing it in his side. Similarly we may be aware of joining hands with the reality of another person in the exchange of peace.

Have you believed because you have seen me?

Yes, that is true of moments in every Christian's life, and we need not be ashamed of them. We are so built that we need moments of evidence, moments of feeling a presence, but

Blessed are those who have not seen and believed

Such moments are given so that our faith can survive the periods of seeming absence of God, the times when we do not see, yet believe.

Psalm

We are listening to a poet expressing the deepest of all human hopes — that life is not fastened into the boundaries set by time and death. In the words ''my heart is glad, my spirit rejoices, my body shall rest in hope'' there is a very contemporary insight. In a mysterious way religious faith can affect for good every aspect of our being, and can therefore be healing and life-giving.

Third Sunday of Easter

Acts 2:14a, 36–41
1 Peter 1:17–23
Luke 24:13–35
Psalm 116:10–17

Theme How do we proclaim and witness to the risen Christ? By quietly making it obvious that we turn to him as a resource for our lives (Acts), by so conducting our lives that we pursue meaning rather than futile goals (Peter), and by seeking out a living Christian community where both scripture and sacrament nourish us and brings us to an encounter with the risen Christ in our own time (Luke).

First Reading

1 *God has made him Lord and Christ*
2 *They said, "What shall we do?"*
3 *Repent and be baptized*
4 *You shall receive the Holy Spirit*
5 *Save yourself from this crooked generation*

In that sequence, in phrases taken from Acts 2, we see the classic presentation of the Christian message and the response to it. However much we plead that our times and our plural society are quite different from those days, there would seem to be no escaping from some form of proclamation to our age. The question is how it is effectively to be done.

God has made him Lord and Christ

Perhaps beginning with oneself may help. If I am Christian, then presumably Jesus has become Lord of my life. Somehow my life has to communicate (proclaim) that. We tend to shrink from that, yet there are ways to "proclaim" quietly and effectively, as we know well from certain lives around us.

What shall we do?

What are we proclaiming? Simply that his life, lived in a certain place and time, has ultimate significance for my life in my place and time. The response to "What shall we do?" is consciously to bring the life of Our Lord to our own life and let one be measured by the other.

Repent

To let Our Lord's life measure one's own is to discover oneself "repenting," turning from one's own will to another's (his) will. In the simplest of language this will mean changing the pattern of one's life. Some "last" things may have to become "first" things and vice versa. Which these are must be of our own deciding.

Be baptized

In our society and time one may already have been baptized as a child. But baptism is really a life-long process. If I as a baptized adult come to an encounter with Jesus Christ, so that I realize him as Lord in a new and vivid way, then much in my life has to do some "dying" and "rising" again in new ways. That is what baptism is about; we "die" in the water and "rise" from it renewed.

You shall receive the Holy Spirit

If I do come to such an encounter with Jesus Christ, so that I wish to make him Lord of my life, then I will be conscious that he too responds to me in the encounter. I will be conscious of a new attitude, a new "spirit" guiding me and leading me toward what and whom I wish to become.

Save yourself from this crooked generation

There is an interesting contemporary ring to this. If Peter sees this as part of the act of repenting, then what can this mean for us? Is there here an acknowledgement that repentance cannot be complete as merely an individual act but must also be the adoption of a critical and evaluating stance toward the social issues of our time? What is "crooked" (unjust) about certain aspects of my society?

Second Reading   *The time of your exile*

Such a description of human life has been echoed by many Christian writers, among them C.S. Lewis. Like all images it can be stretched to a self-defeating point. At best it brings out the fact that reality as we experience it in daily life is only the shadow of a much greater reality. The tragedy is that in Western culture we insist on thinking of that greater reality (God and the kingdom of God) as itself unreality! But on earth in the city of humanity we are "exiled" from our true home in the city of God. In many such ways our "exile" has been expressed. The image of life as exile becomes unhelpful only when it is used to justify a retreat by Christians from involvement in the questions and challenges of their society and time.

Conduct yourselves with fear

"Fear" means, of course, a fear of God, a sense of responsibility and accountability to an ultimate authority and ultimate evaluation. The phrase "conduct yourselves" brings us back to the question about proclamation and witnessing brought up in the Acts passage. The most effective evangelizing and witnessing for Christ is the conducting of our lives. This is as true in the twentieth as in the first century. What might be some marks of that conduct? A sense of being ransomed?

Ransomed from futile ways

Could this mean that one is given the wisdom to see the "futility" of certain aspects of modern life — consumerism, escapism (in such things as endless TV watching), nuclearism (the futility of a never-ending arms race)?

Through him you have confidence . . . your faith and hope are in God

Confidence, not as something based on self-importance or self-justification, but on the knowledge that one is accepted by a loving creator whose destiny for creation is resurrection. On this one's faith and hope are based, and by this one's existence is empowered.

Third Reading   *A village named Emmaus about seven miles from Jerusalem*

To be a Christian in this age means that one is almost certainly living in, or deeply affected by, today's urban world (Jerusalem). To urban souls there comes at times the wish to return to the simplicity and purity (real or imagined) of the village (Emmaus).

> *Talking and discussing . . . Jesus drew*
> *near . . . but their eyes were kept from*
> *recognizing him*

Very often today many feel that in various ways Christ has been taken from them, as did these two disciples. Many feel that Christian faith and life have deeply changed. Many questions have appeared. Sophistication challenges a remembered simplicity. Familiar liturgies have been replaced by seeming innovations. Not only the rules of personal morality seem different, but a whole set of social moral questions clamour for solution. In the seemingly new reality of church life, liturgy, and moral questions, many cannot "see Jesus drawing near." "Their eyes are kept from recognizing him."

> *Are you the only visitor to Jerusalem*
> *who does not know the things that have*
> *happened?*

There is anger here, just as there is anger in many Christians at "the church." "It" doesn't understand. "It" doesn't care. "It" doesn't have the old answers.

> *Some women of our company . . . had*
> *even seen a vision of angels who said*
> *that he was alive*

However, within today's church there are also those who "have seen a vision." For those men and women Christ is alive in the contemporary situation, but his voice has to be heard and his touch felt and his face recognized in new ways. That is precisely what the risen Lord now sets about making possible on the Emmaus road.

> *He interpreted to them . . . the scrip-*
> *tures . . . concerning himself*

In recent years there has been a growing realization across the church. Its claims on Christian attention and concern for issues such as justice within our society and beyond it — peace in the world and racial strife, to name only a few — must be seen to be based on scripture. When this is done well, there is a readiness to listen, often a lessening of alienation, an attitude we hear in the invitation given to the stranger who leads them in Bible study. A curiosity is awakened, an attraction felt. They say, "Stay with us."

> *He took the bread, blessed and broke it,*
> *and gave it to them*

Reflection on the scriptures is followed by the breaking of bread together. For two thousand years this is the great double grace offered to us as his followers. Century after century innumerable places, from homes to tiny chapels to vast cathedrals, have become in their turn the Emmaus inn, where scripture is read and expounded and sacrament is shared. As we stand in nervous indecision in our volatile history, fearful of the complexity of our Jerusalem and longing for the simplicity of Emmaus, once again in the profound mingling of scripture and sacrament the risen Christ of our time calls us to encounter.

> *They rose that same hour and returned*
> *to Jerusalem and they found the eleven*

Encountering the risen Christ enables them to choose the challenge of the city rather than the escape of the village. When they do make that choice, they discover in the city a community of faith to which they can give their allegience and from which they can receive grace. The same is true for us, and always will be!

Psalm

Overcome by a sense of gratitude to God, the poet seeks for ways to respond. One way is to express gratitude in real terms (sacrifice). What might that mean for us? Costly giving? Next, the lifting of the cup, for us regular receiving of sacramental grace. Finally, "fulfilling vows in the presence of his people"; for us that might mean living responsibly in our society.

Fourth Sunday of Easter

Acts 2:42–47
1 Peter 2:19–25
John 10:1–10
Psalm 23

Theme Deeply pastoral. We are shown first the marks of a truly pastoral Christian community, marks applicable to any age (Acts). We then see the ultimate pastoral stance of Our Lord, unflinching even in the face of total violence (Peter). Finally we are shown, in the images of the shepherd, the standards for any pastoral role within the church (John).

First Reading   *The people devoted themselves*

"The people" are, of course, that very first generation of Christians who were not yet even called Christian (that was to come later in the far-away Graeco-Roman city of Antioch in Syria). They were gathered mainly in the Jerusalem area, still very much aware of themselves as Jews, still using the temple for worship and gatherings, also most probably using one another's homes for the very necessary mutual solidarity that any emerging movement needs.

As we look back at them, we see an emerging community exhilarated and energized by the wonderful events which have brought it into being. To suggest that such revolutionary fervour cannot last is not cynicism or faithlessness but merely realism. Maoist China eventually realized that revolution cannot be perpetual. There must, of course, be periods of revival, but there must also be periods of quiet consolidation. The same initial blaze of fervour, of deep fellowship, of common sharing, is true of early Islam. It has been true of countless communities in recent centuries, particularly in seventeenth-century England and in twentieth-century North America (Amish, Mennonite, Hutterite).

How can we use this glimpse of those very early years? We can look at the marks of their life and ask what those marks mean for us. Here is a portrait of any truly alive Christian community.

1   *Teaching*
2   *Fellowship*
3   *Breaking of bread*
4   *Prayers*
5   *Were together*
6   *Distributed to all*
7   *Attending the temple together*
8   *Adding to their number*

1   *Teaching.* We are realizing in congregational life that teaching can no longer be the limited methods of Sunday School and sermon. A much greater commitment to teaching the faith is needed and is beginning to be made. Is it among us here? How? What are we willing to do? What resources are available?

2   *Fellowship.* We are realizing that the care and encouragement of those who come into the church is of primary importance. It is a lonely world which most of us come from. Our sensitivity to the newcomer, our ability to make a congregation a fellowship of trust and care, has never been more important.

3 *Breaking of bread.* In almost every Christian tradition there is a recapturing of the essential role of the eucharist, whether or not it is so named. As the Christian communities seek to be places of fellowship, they are discovering that there is no more powerful focus than the sacred meal.

4 *Prayers.* A quiet revolution is going on among many congregations as the centrality of prayer is being discovered. Greater care with the expression of prayer in public worship, the development of prayer chains to lift many known needs in the congregation, the formation of groups for regular prayer in houses or downtown offices — all these elements are forging the prayer revolution.

5 *Were together.* Obviously, an extension of what is said above about fellowship. Today, if congregational life communicates a high quality of fellowship, that very fellowship can give people a sense of community, a feeling, if you will, of being bonded into a tribe where they have a role, significance, friendship, support. In today's society such things are hard to secure.

6 *Distributed to all.* Today it is required of a congregation that it be responsive to the immediate and real needs of its own members and of the surrounding society. It may be by way of such things as neighbourhood residences, resources voluntarily given by professionals within the congregation, or regular and serious participation in local food banks or other such programs.

7 *Attending the temple together.* It may seem obvious to say that regular worship is the central powerhouse of congregational life. It is not obvious to all! Worship is often seen as an option. Some contribute, some teach, some work on projects. We are learning slowly that involvement in worship, especially in eucharistic worship, is mysteriously and immensely powerful in providing the

energy and vision for all our other shared activities. Worship is both literally and metaphorically the Christian's food and drink!

8   *Adding to their number.* Across Christian congregational life there is a dawning realization that Christian faith cannot remain passive, taking its own future for granted. We are realizing the necessity for quiet but intentional witness on the part of all Christians. In the last ten years in North America four out of every five men and women who returned to the life of a Christian church said that they did so because someone who was significant to them in their lives invited them to do so!

What we have done is to take the language used by Luke to describe the Christian community as that first generation knew it. Presumably by the time Luke himself wrote, adaptations were already being made. But just as that description of the early community served as a blueprint for Christians toward the end of the first century, so it can go on serving as a blueprint for Christian communal life, including our own late twentieth-century experience.

Second Reading   *Endures pain while suffering unjustly*

We are listening to Peter at a time of early Christian persecution. He is trying to give meaning to the grim experiences of some by pointing them to the experience of the Lord.

> *He committed no sin . . . when he was*
> *reviled, he reviled not again . . . when*
> *he suffered, he did not threaten*

In places of great injustice, in societies held in the grip of relentless oligarchies, such moral dilemmas are agonizing. When you and those whom you love are ''reviled,'' what do you do as a Christian? When you and others are made to suffer, what do you do as a Christian? These questions are not merely interesting theological issues in such societies! Above every agonized choice stands the pattern of Our Lord who actually broke the cycle of reactive hatred and violence, thus becoming an eternal source of healing in the human predicament (''by his wounds you have been *healed*'').

Third Reading   *He who does not enter the sheepfold by the door*

Much is hidden in this passage. Using the images of shepherding John is contrasting the integrity of Jesus with what he feels is the exploitation and hypocrisy of the surrounding official religion. How can the passage speak to us? We might consider what it can say about the integrity of the role of ministering to others.

Calls sheep by name . . . leads them out . . . goes before them

Here are two roles which must constantly be kept in balance by today's pastor. We might call them ''intimacy and prophecy'' or ''loving and leading.'' On one side, there has got to be communicated a caring for people, an interest in their lives. On the other, there has got to be the resolve to lead them, on the basis of scripture and the Holy Spirit, to reflect on and to act on moral demands which they may neither wish to consider nor to be involved in. That balance is demanding yet unavoidable today if pastor and people are to retain integrity.

I am the door . . . I came that they may have life

God is a God who frees and enables us. Jesus' way was to set gifts free, to help people discover themselves. He was always the door which opened in their lives and led to greater enrichment of their whole being. That quality in the pastoral role, of opening up people's lives and releasing the gifts they didn't even know they had, is invaluable. People are literally given new life.

Psalm

The immortal portrait of the love and leading of God in the images of a shepherd's life. Courageous sure leadership, constant unremitting care, utter dependability, total love. No wonder Christian tradition has always seen in these verses a portrait of Our Lord, shepherd king, an image later to be placed paradoxically beside that of sacrificial lamb.

Fifth Sunday of Easter

Acts 7:55–60
1 Peter 2:2–10
John 14:1–14
Psalm 31:1–8

Theme A common theme in these scriptures is the communication of our faith beyond ourselves. In the death of Stephen we see that the handling of pain and suffering can be an extraordinarily powerful witness in the most unexpected ways (Acts). We hear in Peter's letter how the quality of a Christian congregation can be a means of communicating faith (Peter). Finally Our Lord shows how the ultimate witness to faith is the "way" we ourselves embody the "truth" in "life" (John).

First Reading

The last few Sundays have sounded the euphoria of faith. Resurrection has created joy, hope, faith, mission to others. Suddenly we are reading of the dark side of this early period. We are in a shrieking crowd capable of bringing about a very ugly death. The newly formed Christian community is about to pay the first grim cost of newly discovered faith. Stephen — brilliant, articulate, totally committed — is about to die.

I see the Son of man standing at the right hand of God

This whole scene is to become a pattern for the Christian martyrdom which will come so often in the future. In Stephen it begins to move toward its climax with a witnessing to the kingship of Christ. This is going to be repeated over the next few centuries in Roman amphitheatres. Statements like Stephen's are going to be ascribed to great souls suffering in the tragic wars which are yet to come between Christians themselves in later centuries. Sixteenth-century martyrs standing at stakes before burnings, African martyrs in the nineteenth century preparing to die, even twentieth-century voices such as the cry of Martin Luther King Jr ("I have gone to the mountain. I have seen the glory of the Lord!") are to be patterns for martyrdom. So we are not merely reflecting on a past phenomenon as we read of Stephen. Whatever our political attitudes may be to the various social revolutions in various countries in recent years, the simple fact is that even while we reflect on these scriptures the world has its "Stephens." They lie incarcerated in cells, known and unknown, suffering for their faithfulness to a vision of society whose justice and freedom will in some way reflect the vision of justice we read of in Holy Scripture.

> *The witnesses laid down their garments*
> *at the feet of a young man named Saul*

Here we have one of those great moments of dramatic irony in scripture. Stephen is about to die, Paul the apostle, though he does not realize it, is about to be born from the obsessive bureaucrat named Saul, who is hanging back on the edge of the crowd while it pulverizes Stephen's body. What we are seeing, within months of the events at Calvary and the garden tomb, is the juxtaposition of death and resurrection. Again Christ dies, this time in Stephen, and again Christ is about to rise, this time in Paul. Stephen becomes the tomb of death, Paul the garden of resurrection. The brilliance, faithfulness, and vision being snuffed out in Stephen is going to rise to new life in the brilliance, faithfulness, and vision of the new apostle yet to be formed. That is why this scripture is so very much an Easter scripture, even though it comes to us in the images and sounds of death.

Such things as martyrdom are not the stuff of most of our Christian lives. Martyrdom sounds distant and unreal and exotic to most North American Christians. Can the scripture speak for us at another level?

Lord do not hold this sin against them

In so far as it does involve suffering and pain and death we have much more in common with it. Stephen's way of facing the grim reality — his obvious courage, his lack of hatred — must have deeply affected Saul. Many have been so affected by those whom they have seen face some grim reality with extraordinary courage and lack of bitterness. Sometimes it has brought people to faith in the Christ which they have seen to be so real for the one suffering. Many a "Paul" has been brought into being by the suffering of many a "Stephen."

Second Reading *Long for the pure spiritual milk . . . Come to him [the Lord] . . . rejected by man . . . chosen in God's sight*

These phrases are all doing the same thing. They are asking Christians for a definite commitment rather than a vague adherence. They are a voice asking us to "long for" faith, to see life as a "growing" in that faith rather than just a passive inheriting of it. In fact, they are saying that we should either reject faith or choose it. The common factor is that each choice requires a considered decision.

> *Like living stones be built into a spiritual*
> *house*

A long tradition in Western Christianity has regarded the process of conversion complete when a person decides to be Christian, deciding that "Jesus is Lord." But in recent decades we are realizing that a further step is required — that of grafting that individual Christian life into the life of the Christian community. In Peter's image we are not separate stones, but together we are to form the house which is the people of God.

It is interesting to realize that this image probably came to Peter from the double meaning in his own name Peter (*Petrus* meaning "a stone") which Jesus years before had given him. It is also salutary to observe how easily congregations fall into the trap of thinking of the house of God as the physical bricks and mortar of their church, forgetting that the real house of God and the real stones of God are the men and women and children within and beyond those walls.

To be a holy priesthood

This, of course, is precisely what the whole Christian community is being called to become, and why the nature of worship is changing. Instead of priesthood sanctioning one (ordained) person to act among and for everyone else, priesthood is coming to be seen as enabling everyone in the community to see and act out their own lives as a "ministry," using their own gifts to achieve it.

To offer holy sacrifices

What is a church for? What is a congregation for? It may be a surprising answer to say that it is for celebrating the eucharist. Surely worship is only a means to living life? While this is quite true it is extraordinary how the celebration of the eucharist can become an immensely creative pattern to enable people to live life beyond the liturgy itself. For that reason a congregation can invest a great deal of energy and time in the celebration of the eucharist, without feeling that it is becoming detoured into mere religious activity.

> *You are a chosen race, a royal priesthood, a holy nation, God's own people*

All of which can sound immensely presumptuous on the part of Christians! Yet every one of these titles, if they are to have any reality, has to be earned.

Chosen. How much choosing to make a commitment of one's life to Christ has there been in a congregation? *Priesthood.* How much sense of mutual priesthood is there in the life of a congregation? *Holy nation.* How much commitment is there in the life of a congregation to the quality of the society in which they live and work, how much involvement in its issues? *God's people.* How much sense of solidarity does a congregation have, in contrast to being a fortuitous gathering from time to time of otherwise scattered and disconnected individuals?

> *That you may declare the wonderful deeds*

What is the point of striving for all these qualities? So that something is communicated beyond the congregation itself — the fact that the Christian community has become aware within itself of a source of life-changing grace.

Third Reading

In the first reading we saw Christian faith communicated by the witness of a person in extreme circumstances of pain and violence. We applied that to our own lives in terms of the witness we have seen in others in the face of pain and suffering. In the second reading we thought about how a Christian community communicates faith by the quality of its life. Now we see Our Lord giving us an example of how Christian witness depends on our own living of Christian faith.

> *Jesus said, "I am the way, the truth, and the life*

When someone is aware of us as friend or colleague, then, if we have made any claim to involvement in a Christian community, it is through us that that person sees Christian faith. We are "the way" by which Christian faith makes its claims. We become "the truth" about the Christian life. We become "the life" through which Christian faith is to some degree judged. Any Christian is then ambassador and embodiment of the faith among other people. By him or her Christian faith is measured. This does not take place in argument or discussion. It may never be mentioned! It happens mostly in things noted silently, even subconsciously, as life and relationships are lived out.

> *Believe me for the sake of the works themselves*

Jesus asks this of his disciples. His final appeal is to their observation of his life. He offers it as proof of the integrity of his claim. In a sense we are in the same position before others. As Christians, intentionally or not, we are the "sign" of our professed faith. Not only is Our Lord asking Philip to accept Jesus' ongoing life as evidence of the reality of his claims, he is also pointing out to all of us that our lives are, to use today's language, ''the bottom line'' when it comes to providing evidence of our faith. However much we would wish it otherwise, people believe in us and in what we stand for on the basis of our ''works.'' The mark of true belief in Jesus as Lord, as he points out to us, is that we ''do the works'' which he does — we reflect something of the quality of his life in ours.

Psalm

For the Christian this is a song of Jesus Christ as the resource for living life. There will be ambiguous and complex situations (''the net secretly set for me''). There will be value judgements to be made (''worthless idols''). In all this we realize our vulnerable humanity (my affliction). Yet we also know that we are accepted and forgiven by Christ (''you know my distress''), and therefore growth and victory are possible (''not . . . in the power of the enemy'').

Sixth Sunday of Easter

Acts 17:22–31
1 Peter 3:13–22
John 14:15–21
Psalm 66:7–18

Theme We are present when the Christian claims are articulated by Paul to the sophistication and pluralism of Athens, a place very similar to our society (Acts). Peter, speaking to us as Christians in any age, emphasizes that our living of Christian faith gives integrity to our profession of it. He points out that our baptism, which physically brings us out of water, is a spiritual resource for helping us to rise above life's circumstances (Peter). The Gospel re-emphasizes that loving God and living obediently to God's commands must go together. Without obedience love is unreal (John).

First Reading

As we saw last Sunday, we are at a stage when the Easter faith is being communicated and its reception is varied. We have moved from the euphoric acceptance following Peter's sermon (Easter) to the savage rejection of Stephen's witness. Once again we are spectators to another moment when a Christian voice tries to communicate the Easter faith. By now Paul has moved across half the empire. He finds himself in the heart of that empire's intellectual life. Paul stands in Athens.

In the middle of the Areopagus

Here is the public area where people can engage others in whatever communication they wish. Immediately we have an image of our own pluralistic society and its media. Everything here is in a sense "value free," to use modern language. There is both exhilaration and freedom about it, but there can also be chilling detachments, as we well know. Most likely Paul felt both.

You are very religious

So are we as a culture. As with the Greeks our religious tendancy covers an immensely wide spectrum. There is fundamentalist and aggressively evangelical religion. There is socially concerned religion. There is a diffuse sense of the religious arising from the terror and wonder of our age and its achievements. Possibly we may be living in one of the most religious periods in recent centuries.

"I found an altar to an unknown god"

That phrase describes much of our religion. There is in one way a ring of sadness about it. In today's world there is a deep haunted longing for God more than a strong sense of divine presence. As our society moves into ever increasing complexity, we have a disturbing sense of knowing less and less about most things, and acknowledging this is inevitable. We are tempted to feel that reality as a whole is unknowable or, in religious terms, that intimacy and relationship with God is impossible.

> *What you worship as unknown, this I*
> *proclaim to you*

At first hearing, Paul's statement has a ring of the rabid fundamentalist, an attitude of "You have only questions, I have all the answers." But a Christian always runs this risk, because the great Christian claim is that God, the unknowable, has made Godhood known in Jesus Christ. Here in first-century Athens that is what Paul is trying to say. He does not have an easy task — as indeed is true for those who wish to commend Jesus Christ today.

The God who made the world

Paul begins with God as creator, probably because he feels he will be on common ground with his listeners. Today even the assumption of a creator cannot be assumed to be a common belief in a crowd, but it is still reasonably useful and safe ground.

> *Yet he is not far from each one of us*

Paul then moves into the idea of the God felt within human experience. Again he is trying to find common ground with his listeners.

> *Now he commands all . . . everywhere,*
> *to repent . . . he will judge the world*

Suddenly Paul jumps on to much less common ground. God is moral. Human life is accountable. God makes demands on the human. God is suddenly more demanding and inconvenient than a merely fascinating philosophical concept! Pastorally we all know people who like to "discuss religion," as a kind of mental jogging!

A man he has appointed . . . by raising him from the dead

At this point Paul must have taken a deep breath before plunging into his last climactic statement. It's important for us to realize what he was trying *not* to be heard to say, and here we are on necessary contemporary ground as well. The Greeks, like many late twentieth century people, were perfectly familiar with resurrection as an interesting idea, usually found in poetic or mythic form. But here was a man passionately presenting resurrection to them as a reality, precisely dated, given a face and a name! Why that is important to emphasize is that this is precisely what Christian faith is saying to modern society.

Second Reading

In this scripture we are in a later period than Paul's day. For the first time resistance is setting in to Christian claims, unpleasant things are beginning to be experienced. Peter is trying to outline some attitudes which may be helpful in a complex and unpredictable situation.

Even if you do suffer

There is a grim hint that it was becoming more and more likely that Christians would encounter suffering.

Make a defence of the hope in you with gentleness and reverence

The likelihood of anyone "calling us to account" for our faith in our society is remote, at least in the sense and circumstances of those early days. Yet we would be wrong to assume that there are not more subtle ways in which this can happen. We all have a tendancy to avoid being seen to make "a big deal" of any subject. Detachment, "hanging loose," "being cool" are desirable traits in our culture. Yet there is immense need for Christians to be able to respond attractively yet seriously when opportunity presents itself, intended or not, to discuss faith. Certainly there will be those who think this is a trifle weird, but let us not fear to be thought intriguingly and gracefully weird!

Keep your conscience clear

Peter is pointing out a timeless fact, that the most effective way to commend our faith is by our life-style, our perceived actions and objectives, seen and shared in work and community by others. Whether for first-century or twentieth-century Christians, the ultimate vehicle for demonstrating the integrity of our religion is the integrity of our lives.

> *Being put to death but made alive . . .*
> *Noah, during the building of the ark*
> *. . . baptism now saves you*

In three linked images Peter speaks of dying and rising. Christ goes under the waters of death and returns. Noah rises in the ark above a drowning world. Baptism takes us under waters and above them again. All three images are a single truth, timelessly true. As a Christian, even though I live in a world that is drowning and dying — which I sometimes experience inside myself as frustration, fear, anxiety — I possess a grace from Jesus Christ my Lord, which empowers me in my struggle to rise above that drowning and dying.

Third Reading   *If you love me, you will keep my commandments*

Again is sounded the theme of the necessity for reality in Christian allegiance. Profession of faith in and love for God are tested by perceived conduct.

The Spirit of truth . . . dwells with you and will be in you

Here is the great truth that Western spirituality has always found difficult. God is not a distant deity to be placated and to grant forgiveness. The spirit of God is already within our human spirits. The light shines in our darkness, to use another image. We may wish to reach back to Paul's saying in Athens, "God is not far from each one of us, for in him we live and move and have our being" (that last half he quoted from a Greek poet).

He who has my commandments and keeps them, he (or she) it is who loves me

Once again the same theme is sounded this Sunday. Love is tested by our lives. Love of God and obedience of a will other than our own go together. Knowledge — "having" God's commandments — is not enough. Only the keeping of them is relevant. Only by a lived faith is a relationship formed between humanity and God. After all, human relationships, if they are to become eventually rich and creative, depend on actions beyond mere protestations of love. Thus we read of our relationship with God, "He who . . . keeps my commandments . . . I will love him and manifest myself to him."

Psalm

A song of recently experienced grim events. People have been "tried." They have become aware of "heavy burdens." They have felt in "over their heads." They have "come through fire." All these are universal human experiences. We even use these phrases about life today. Yet, now that these things are over, (for now?) there is not merely relief that they are over, not merely a feeling of mere survival. Instead there is an intense expression of thanksgiving to, and trust in, God. There is a sense that survival has been possible because of grace given. These thoughts and feelings of thanks, trust, and grace received are frequently missing from contemporary human experience.

Seventh Sunday of Easter

Acts 1:6–14
1 Peter 4:12–14,
5:6–11
John 17:1–11
Psalm 68:1–10

Theme These scriptures can be seen as a trilogy. The Christian community is being given its commission by its Lord as he ascends. Responsibility passes to them (Acts). The same community at a later date is being instructed in ways to behave and function in a difficult period (Peter). In the Gospel the earliest form of the community, the apostolic band, is being prayed for by its Lord. In that prayer we also hear his prayer for us in our time as a Christian community (John).

First Reading

Lord, will you at this time restore the kingdom to Israel?

It's a strange and ambiguous question. What kind of kingdom is the questioner hoping for? Is it a question about the chances of Israel developing an empire again? Or is it a question about Israel as a society showing some aspects of the kingdom of God in the quality of its life and institutions? The question is important because Christians should always be asking it in some form in their own time. Healthy Christian faith will not look for a detached God to suddenly transform history and society, but will ask the question, Lord of our age, what elements of your kingdom do you wish us to build into society as an offering of our energy and gifts? Asking the question in those terms is also bringing out the importance of the words "at this time." Christian faith does not merely place the kingdom of God at, or even beyond, some end point of history, but also commits itself to building what can be achieved "at this time."

> *You shall receive power . . . you shall be*
> *my witnesses*

Our Lord at this point is transferring responsibility for future initiatives to the community which his life and death and resurrection have formed. To be a "witness" does not merely mean one who has seen something, but someone who begins to embody and communicate certain new realities because of what he or she has seen. Of crucial importance here is that this whole passage is a dialogue between every generation of Christians and their Lord.

> *He was lifted up, and a cloud took him*
> *out of their sight*

The very clear message being communicated is that a direct, tangible, visible presence of Our Lord is over. The mode of his presence is now in his community. His hands become our hands, his feet our feet. That does not mean an absence of Our Lord till the end of time. It means his presence is in and among his people. The responsibility of this is not easy to accept, and Luke has to emphasize it by having the message voiced.

> *Why do you stand gazing up into*
> *heaven?*

It is a timeless and necessary question. Christians are not a primitive tribe waiting for something to drop from the sky. Most certainly there is that which is above and beyond us. Not for a moment can Christian faith deny transcendence. But the whole point of Our Lord's work is that the transcendent has reached down, touching and entering the human, and working through the human.

They returned to Jerusalem

If we take Jerusalem as an image of "the city," the urban world which is the context of most of our lives, we see the community immediately acting out their understanding of the message received. They head into the reality in which they must now be witnesses. For most of them it is an unfamiliar and rather threatening reality, as it can be for us. The church as a whole has found it difficult to come to terms with the city, its transience, its pluralism, its detachment, its secularism.

They went up to the upper room . . . all with one accord devoted themselves to prayer

Their behaviour communicates that they thought of themselves very much as a community, not as a gathering of individuals. They had shared experiences both joyful and agonizing. From these experiences they had caught a vision. From the vision they had discovered a vocation. That sequence is not a bad description of what is necessary if a congregation today is to be truly alive.

Second Reading

Something of the same theme echoes here. A community is being given directions on how to behave, how to survive. Again, we ask, what does the passage say to us as a Christian generation?

*Do not be surprised at the fiery ordeal
which comes upon you, as though
something strange were happening to
you*

Language like that may seem melo-
dramatic for the situation facing today's church, yet there
is a sense in which it can be applied. It has become common-
place to think of our time as extremely difficult, complex,
and demanding. Religious faith is moving through a very
unpredictable and almost undefinable stage. Human life,
although surrounded by achievements, is riddled with self-
doubts and with a deep dread of those very achievements.
In at least one terrible sense we do realize "a fiery ordeal
(nuclear) coming upon us" if we are not extremely careful.
All this gives us a feeling of being fatally threatened. This
we experience in common with that early Christian generation, though of course for different reasons.

*Rejoice in so far as you share Christ's
sufferings*

In what sense can we see ourselves co-
operating with Christ as the Lord of history as he wrestles
to bring that history to the consummation he wills for it.
His involvement in time and history was costly. If we feel
that faithfulness to him today is costly, how can we see it
as sharing in Christ's sacrifice?

*If you are reproached for the sake of
Christ*

In our society one is rarely if ever
attacked for Christian faith. But contemporary life can be
adept at the patronizing remark, the implication that our

religion is at best a harmless, even charming, idiosyncrasy and, at worst, a rather unrealistic neurotic strand in our makeup.

> *Humble yourselves under the mighty hand of God . . . all your anxieties*

We are to place ourselves and our age and society within the context of another and greater will and purpose.

> *Be sober, be watchful . . . the devil prowls*

In a frantic, nervous, and anxious age we are to live with as much calm and serenity as possible. For instance, ages such as Peter's and ours are much given to seeking gratification of the various appetites in food, sex, clothes, speed, security, fame. Paradoxically one can be devoured by the appetite. To speak of sobriety is to challenge rampant appetite. We have given away the fine term *puritan* to those who sneer at it. But all balanced human life needs an element of what that word means.

Third Reading

This time a community is being prayed for, as its leader prepares for a change in his relationship with it. Jesus is on the edge of his Passion. In a deep sense Our Lord is praying for us.

> *Glorify thy Son that the Son may glorify thee*

That could be the prayer of each one of us. ''God, give me some of your glory, so that I in my living may give you glory.''

> *I glorified thee on earth, having accomplished the work which thou gavest me to do*

As good a definition as one can get of what our lives are about. A reminder too that "giving glory" to God is not necessarily done only in worship. Being able to have a sense of vocation about what we do in and with our lives is to give God glory. We see something of this in the famous statement of a great craftsman. "God," said Stradivarius, "could not make the violins of Stradivarius without the fingers of Stradivarius."

> *I am glorified in them*

It is easy to miss the tremendous affirmation of our humanity in that phrase. Consider how pathetic and even contemptible the lives of the early disciples could be at times. Consider the unworthiness we are only too well aware of in ourselves. Yet Our Lord says that he is glorified in us! What immense things that could do for our sense of self-worth if we really hear it.

> *They are in the world. Holy Father, keep them in thy name . . . that they may be one*

They were in a very harsh and demanding world, as we are. John was a realist about life. He saw the world as God's creation, yet he also saw it as a kind of demanding tyrant wrestling with God for our allegiance. To be kept in God's name, as Our Lord prays we may be, could be always to see our essential being, our inner nature, as belonging to God before it belongs to anything else, to any cause, to any temptation, even to our own self.

That they may be one

There is the great prayer which has always been a challenge to Christians. How is the Christian experience to express a unity in the face of different histories, different cultures, different temperaments? Yet here also, perhaps, Our Lord is praying for us individually, that our faith in him may enable each of us to "be one," to retain our integrity, to "get things together" in a deeply spiritual sense, above all to remain at one with him in a life-long relationship.

Psalm

There is of course the repeated image of the Lord of the heavens. But that Lord is not detached from the human situation, especially its pain — orphans, widowhood, prisoners, the poor. God is a God who can be encountered in the wildernes in which human experience often finds itself.

The Day of Pentecost

Acts 2:1–21
1 Corinthians
12:3b–13
John 20:19–23
Psalm 104:25–35

Theme Naturally, the theme is that of God's Holy Spirit. The first Pentecost has much to say to our sense of living at the end of an age in which we see around us a rich and varied spirituality (Acts). The gifts of Christian spirituality come in many ways, none of which should be dismissed or belittled by the others (Corinthians). The Holy Spirit comes not merely to individuals but to the gathered community (John).

First Reading *The day of Pentecost . . . they were all together*

Christians are well aware that the Holy Spirit can enter into individual experience in a life-changing way. We also know that there is an instinctive urge to share such an experience with others, to become part of some Christian worshipping community. It is as if community is the natural setting for Christian growth and practice. There is a hint here that at least part of the immense power of the first Pentecost derives from the early Christians being in community, gathered in a particular place. That in itself is a powerful message to Christians today. More and more in the last few decades we have discovered that good and great things happen in congregations which have begun to see themselves not as a number of separate individuals who happen to use a building in common at regular intervals, but as a community whose lives are at least to some degree interwoven and mutually caring.

A sound came from heaven like the rush of a mighty wind

It is easy to forget that this is not a fortuitous example of mass euphoria. This moment is an expected rendezvous. The risen Lord actually warned them to await it, to expect it. What rendezvous with the Holy Spirit do we expect individually? What rendezvous with the Holy Spirit do we expect as a congregation? Expectation was then, and is always, a most important factor in Christian life.

Like a wind . . . tongues as of fire

Notice how we always have to grope for metaphor to describe spiritual experience. Luke is not saying that each one in that room saw flames. He is saying that everyone knew very well that the person next to him or her was on fire with joy and energy and a sense of the Lord's presence!

They began to speak in other tongues

Why? Because sometimes our sense of the presence of God is so strong and so sweeping that there simply are no words to express what we want to express. For some of us the option will be silence, for others a groping for language, for some a total releasing of themselves in gesture and sound that can be heard as song or chant or even moan. Some can and do dismiss this as babble. Some can be offended and embarrassed, but the person who has experienced the spiritual moment has a deep sense of peace and joy as it passes. What many have realized in recent decades is that ''tongues'' can be a very real spiritual gift. They may be given once or repeatedly. They may be experienced over a period of one's life and then be withdrawn. Christians as a whole have learned neither to minimize nor to absolutize the experience of tongues. It is one of the many gifts of the Holy Spirit, and no Christian is necessarily the recipient of all.

> *What does this mean? They are filled with new wine!*

It is hard to imagine a more ironic attempt at dismissal. Because, of course, that is precisely what Christian energy and joy and purpose do come from, the new wine of Christ.

> *In the last days, God declares, I will pour out my spirit*

There is a very real sense in which we live in "last days." To believe this one does not have to expect the world's end momentarily (though we ourselves possess the means to bring that about). A long period of human civilization is ending, as we know it. The shape of the future is very confused. In such "last days" there is a deep and widespread sense of the "spiritual," of the wonder and terror of existence as being somehow beyond our human control.

> *Wonders in the heavens . . . signs on the earth . . . the sun turned into darkness*

We live at such a time. We know that the "wonder" may be a satellite curving across the night sky, a huge inhabited laboratory tumbling through space, but that makes it no less a wonder. We see signs which again we can identify — the terrible fires of a nuclear reactor out of control, the fearful deserts created by industrial toxic wastes — but they are no less "signs." All tell us of "a day of the Lord" in the sense that we live as human beings who are answerable for our role within the domain of that same Lord.

Second Reading   *Varieties of gifts, but the same Spirit . . . varieties of service, but the same Lord . . . varieties of working, but it is the same God who inspires*

Paul is only too aware of something that would happen among Christians again and again. He knew that, because the human experience of the presence of God is an intense and arresting experience, human nature would very easily make the mistake of regarding one's own personal experience as the only valid one, or at least make the mistaken claim that one gift is more important or more essential or even more "spiritual" than another. This he tries to prevent by a repeated warning. He didn't fully succeed, as we well know from attitudes in some Christian congregations!

To each . . . for the common good

Again and again we are being taught this. Christian experience is not a fully lived-out experience until it is set in community. In community our claims to spirituality are tested, sometimes even harshly; yet even this testing probes our spirituality for reality and forces it to mature.

Of the many gifts Paul mentions we take two for comment.

Gifts of healing

The concept of healing and the many realities hidden within it have returned to Christian experience in recent years. We cannot go into the complex story of these mysteries being lost in Western Christianity in recent centuries, and of the "ministry of healing" now becoming accepted but still regarded as a gift limited to a very few, often centred in a particular parish or person or residential community. What is happening today is a recognition that the Christian community itself can assume a healing role in its members' lives in may ways — by actual deeds of helping or gifts which assist, by corporate (chain) prayer, by visitation or encouragement or simple friendship. Again it is being recognized that, while some men and women seem to possess a very real and special healing gift, all of us have the capacity to develop a presence that brings healing. We can have gifts of touch, of "being with," of listening, of comforting, to name some.

[Gift to] distinguish between Spirits

In an age like this, of varied and often very intense spiritual experience, it is often necessary for us to try to evaluate our own spiritual experiences and those of others. There can be dark and unhealthy spiritual manifestations which, if unchecked and unquestioned, can be damaging to the person and to the Christian community. There are those, sometimes through training and sometimes by natural gift, who can be of immense help in this area, provided that we are prepared to accept such help.

Third Reading   *The doors being shut, for fear*

First we hear this phrase as a tragic comment on some Christians and some congregations. Their doors, psychological, organizational, and spiritual are shut. Very often this is "for fear" — fear of change, fear of what will make demands or require some growing, fear of a call to the new and untried.

For fear of the Jews

It may seem obvious, but for some terrible twentieth-century reasons it is becoming imperative in contemporary preaching to point out certain realities about New Testament times. John wrote at a time when Judaism, struggling to survive and find itself, saw the deviation that was to become Christianity as a threat (quite correctly!) and, of course, the attitude was reciprocated. Many times in John's Gospel "the Jews" are the enemy. We need to be reminded that those behind the door were also Jews, including him who came with the salutation, "Shalom."

> *He breathed on them, and said, "Receive the Holy Spirit"*

It is interesting that this moment of receiving does not involve intense response such as speaking in tongues. The risen Christ is making very plain that the task of embodying the Father's will in the world is now passing to them. They will now embody it personally and, more significantly, as a community. The very first task assigned to them is the sensitive but so necessary task of evaluating the actions and motivations and visions — the spiritualities — of the community. That thought links back to the same thought in today's Epistle reading.

Psalm

Notice how we are immediately reminded that the work of the Holy Spirit is more than personal. In some sense it is involved in the renewal of everything! Renewal of the environment ("earth full of your creatures"), of resource distribution ("there move the ships"). All things are dependant, including our humanity ("All look to you . . . all die"). All are renewed by the Spirit of God. God is all in all.

Trinity Sunday

Deuteronomy 4:32–40
2 Corinthians
13:5–14
Matthew 28:16–20
Psalm 33:1–12

Theme The many-faceted nature of God. We first reflect on God as Lord of history, also its critic and judge (Deuteronomy). Then we consider God as being within human experience and human relationships, through the indwelling of Jesus Christ in our humanity (Corinthians). Finally we reflect on God, again through Christ, giving his Spirit to a community, not because it is deserving or perfect, but because God chooses to work with our humanity (Matthew).

First Reading

Know therefore this day, and lay it to your heart, that the Lord is God

This majestic passage is originally addressed to Israel. Knowing this, we must ask how it speaks to us. Remembering the title of this Sunday helps. The "Trinity" has always been a kind of shorthand for something which confronts the human mind and heart when it tries to conceive the nature of God. The very word *God* is deceptively simple. We might well remember that the word *God* merely serves to name the ultimate mystery. Having a word, a name, can delude us into thinking that we somehow understand and even control that ultimate mystery. It is to avoid such an illusion that to this day orthodox Judaism does not even utter the name of God when it occurs in the reading of scripture.

Ask now of the days that are past

Since the ultimate mystery of God cannot be engaged, we then, as it were, go looking for signs of God's presence. The writer of Deuteronomy is saying, "Look for evidence of a purpose in your history as a people." This way is not the only option. We could have had chosen for today a passage which says, "Look for evidence of a design and a presence in nature itself."

Know therefore . . . lay it to your heart
that the Lord is God in heaven above
and on the earth beneath

To look in our history for design and purpose, thus discerning the presence of God in it, is not to claim some moral or cultural superiority or to claim some divine approval for one's own political system or way of life. This needs to be said because there is always the temptation. The moment we give in to that temptation, the more dangerously we begin to assume divine approval for our actions and our policies.

To look in our history is to "know" God as immeasurably greater than any particular history. To recognize this is to be released from any illusions about one's own way or system. If God is "Lord of heaven above and of earth beneath," then God is Lord of ours and of all histories. As such, God is both the inspiration of, and critic and judge of, human history. In other words, to say that God is "Lord of heaven and of earth beneath" is again to send language in pursuit of ultimate mystery. It is striving to express what the hymn "Immortal, invisible, God only wise" is reaching for. Like all our thinking and all our expression it partially succeeds, but only partially. That is the most important realization of all.

You shall keep his statutes

Here is the healthy element of warning in Judaism which keeps it and us from an arrogant and un-self-critical view of ourselves. Knowledge of God is not mere knowing. There is a relationship between the divine and the human in which the human is the lesser. We are fallible and flawed. There is in us a potential for illusion, evil, and tragedy. Therefore we are called to obedience.

Second Reading　*Examine yourselves . . . test yourselves*

To do so requires discipline. Self-examination is best undertaken with the help of a wise experienced person who can be one's trusted counsellor and what is often called "spiritual director." Some men and women have a particular gift for this. We are only beginning to rediscover this role in the Christian community. If we cannot have such a resource the next best thing is to have some quiet times either with a trusted group who wish to do the same or on our own. Sometimes having a simple pattern to refer to may help. One can move down through the confession in the eucharist asking, "Have I . . .?" or "How have I. . .?" We can do the same with the Lord's Prayer, examining and testing ourselves on the basis of each phrase. These are two ways among many.

Jesus Christ is in you

The wonder and power of the Christian experience is that the Spirit which energizes creation and history is, through Jesus Christ, also at work within you and me, likewise energizing and guiding. It does not take us over. It leaves us free, but it acts with us and for us when we align our wills with his.

Agree with one another . . . live in peace

Paul is writing to a community racked with dissension. The reason why this letter has become very contemporary for Christians is that there are so many different hopes, visions, intentions, expectations, methods in today's experience that dissension is very possible in any worshipping community. Paul knew that such things cannot be ignored. They must be named and dealt with in the trust and hope that the Spirit within the community as a whole can stand dealing with issues in a way that is at once both loving and honest, hopeful and realistic, gentle but strong.

Grace . . . love . . . fellowship

This totally familiar blessing can also be a short but magnificent definition of what we look to a Christian community to be. A place where grace is found, where love is experienced, where fellowship is shared.

Third Reading   *The eleven disciples*

First God's Spirit is seen in history (Deuteronomy), then in each of us (Corinthians), and now in a community. God's Holy Spirit is at work in many ways. This, too, is what that very cerebral sounding word *Trinity* is about.

Notice the word *eleven*. To be complete, ''eleven'' should be ''twelve.'' But of course one (Judas) has broken the circle, smashed and betrayed the image. This says to us that there never was some golden age when the church was perfect (''twelve''). It is always a weakened ''eleven.''

Go therefore and make disciples

Being "eleven," being flawed and already betrayed, does not for a moment mean that they are not to be the chosen instrument by which the Lord's work will continue to be done. And so it will be to the end of time. There never was, is not, and never will be the perfect human instrument for God to work through, other than Our Lord Jesus Christ.

When they saw him, they worshipped him; but some doubted

Again we are given a supremely honest and realistic portrait of a human community. If this was some mythical saga, replete with golden memories, all would be bowed in rapt adoration. But as in any group, any congregation, there are degrees of involvement, many differing motives, lots of hidden agenda. Some worship, some doubt. But the interesting thing is that they are there together, worshippers and doubters, fervent and faint-hearted. That is precisely what congregational life is about. It has room for many stages of the Christian journey. A congregation is not only a place for children, youth, adults, and elderly in the physical sense, but for any such inner stage of the Christian pilgrimage. A forty-five year old may be just beginning or just beginning again.

I am with you always

Herein lies the reason why it is possible for this flawed, frequently betrayed, and betraying thing called the church to continue. Because it is not merely itself. It is human, most human, but not merely human. Our Lord who died and rose to give it life, is in it and, by his promise, always will be.

Psalm

Interestingly the first image of God in the song is of a people, a community at worship. There are many kinds of instruments. Can we think of them as images of many human gifts? God is then shown as involved in the search for justice ("loves righteousness and justice"). God is Lord of the created orders ("stores the depths of the sea"). God is involved in the ongoing process of international relationships ("the will of the nations").

Sunday Between 19 and 25 June

Genesis 28:10–17
Romans 5:12–19
Matthew 10:24–33
Psalm 91:1–10

Theme The theme of setting out on a new journey is common to these passages, even though it is less obvious in the Epistle. Certainly Jacob sets out on what will be a life long journey [Genesis]. And Paul can be heard telling his readers that, because of what has been achieved by Jesus Christ, human nature itself has now begun a new phase or journey [Romans]. In the Gospel we listen as Our Lord gives those who would be his disciples a realistic description of what the conditions of service will be [Matthew].

First Reading *Jacob left Beer-Sheba and went towards Haran*

Our beginnings are difficult, sometimes dangerous, and often fearful. This is true whether we are speaking of our birth or of the many occasions when we must begin another stage of life's journey. We may have to change direction, maybe even retrace our steps. Consider some of the necessary changes that almost all of us have experienced. The move from home to early school, and graduation from high school or university. The plan to travel on one's own or with a friend. The walk down an aisle with another human being who will be a companion on the journey. The decision to take a certain job, or later to change to another. The realization that certain stages in the journey are unavoidable and affect on one's deepest being. The passing from early adult life to early middle age, facing and accepting retirement, coming to terms with the limits of life as we know it. All such changes can be linked with the deceptively simple statement that Jacob left Beer-sheba.

Jacob went towards Haran

Does Haran sound familiar? It's where Abraham began part of his journey to the south. Now his grandson makes Haran a destination on his journey north. This may serve to remind us of something very ironic, particularly about youthful journeying. Very often in youth we grimly determine to break new directions, to assert independence, to prove ourselves different; yet without knowing it we may cover ground that is very familiar to earlier generations of our family. By going in a certain direction, travelling in a certain way, or following apparently self-created goals, we may be proving quite unconsciously that we are indeed the children of our parents and grandparents! One of the delights of later life is discovering that the new and private roads we so earnestly explored were in fact familiar, at least in part, to those from whom we thought we were so effectively diverging. For many of us "Haran" can be an image of such discovery. It was, I think, T.S. Eliot who observed that when we come to the end of our exploring we sometimes discover that the place is none other than that from which we set out.

> *He came to a certain place and stayed*
> *there that night*

The place is as yet unnamed. There is
a hint of being anywhere and nowhere, maybe even a little
lost. The early stages of the journey are the most insecure.
One's equipment is unproved, oneself untested, experience
minimal. The very statement "because the sun had set" is
an image of danger, vulnerability, and fear.

> *He put* [*the stone*] *under his head, lay*
> *down to sleep . . . and he dreamed*

The stone can be a very simple and
effective image of the homelessness we can experience on
our journeying. We are no longer surrounded by the
familiar, the loving, the caring. Those soft elements of life
have for the present been left behind. Our sleep is restless
for the same reason, our dreams sometimes troubled.

> *He dreamed there was a ladder set up on*
> *the earth, and the top of it reached to*
> *heaven*

Jacob's dream is essentially good, the
kind of dream we might do well to possess ourselves if we
could. Its images are integrative. They bring many things
together, things which are very much torn apart in our
culture and contemporary thinking. There is a ladder connecting earth and heaven. In the modern mind that con-
nection is broken. The world of earth, the world of space-
time, has for our culture become the only reality. Heaven
is at best a concept for those who wish to hold it, at worst
an illusion. Francis Thompson, the nineteenth-century
English poet, used the same image to express the integration of the world of space-time with a surrounding and
greater reality.

O World invisible, we view thee,
O world intangible, we touch thee,
O world unknowable, we know thee,
Inapprehensible, we clutch thee!

The angels keep their ancient places; —
Turn but a stone, and start a wing!
'Tis ye, 'tis your estranged faces,
That miss the many-splendour'd thing.

But (when so sad thou canst not sadder)
Cry; — and upon thy so sore loss
Shall shine the traffic of Jacob's ladder
Pitched betwixt Heaven and Charing Cross.

Behold, the Lord stood above it

At the apex of the ladder stands God. Modern thinking is sometimes so overwhelmed by the seeming magnitude of contemporary issues that concepts of God are diminished. God, while seeming to be an allowable, helpful hypothesis for some, can only with difficulty be thought of by many as Lord of creation, its source and its enabler, its beginning and end.

I am the Lord, the God of Abraham your father, and the God of Isaac

Even when we are capable of conceiving God as the Lord of creation, we have great difficulty believing that this Lord can offer any intimacy of relationship to us. For Jacob, God is a present and intimate reality, within whose will and purpose Jacob himself has meaning. This is one of the great convictions of Judaism. We see it expressed again and again in scripture, especially in the Psalms. Two modern film makers, Ingmar Bergman and Woody Allen, though very different in their approach, express this great biblical conviction by constant implication in their movies.

> *Your descendants shall be like the dust of the earth . . . and by you and your descendants shall all the families of the earth be blessed*

Notice how this vision of the future is not seen in terms of power. At first it sounds like that, but the vision turns into one of service. Israel will be both among the nations and also present for the nations, its life a contribution to theirs, its gifts shared with theirs.

> *Surely God is in this place*

For Jacob, though he is no longer at home, God is present. We very badly need Jacob's awareness of a God whose presence we will not leave merely because we journey. Jacob has a deep sense of place. Where he is, God will be; therefore Jacob will be able to function and his existence will have meaning. Today our humanity needs a strong awareness of the presence of God with us, precisely because our sense of place, our sense of where we are, is fragile. For many, God was present in past times, past words, past forms, past customs, but has been left in that lovely, easier, finer past. We, on the other hand, have travelled far through great and terrible events and through vast changes. We do not know where we are, and we feel that God is not with us. We very badly need Jacob's sense of a God who travels with us.

Second Reading *If many died through one man's trespass, much more have the grace of God and the free gift in the grace of that one man Jesus Christ abounded for many*

In that single sentence lies one of the great expressions of Paul's thought. Two facts are put side by side and contrasted. Two mysteries are linked — the mystery of human sin and the mystery of Christ's grace. Somehow and at some point in our creation (for Paul the focus of this is Adam, the symbol of our humanity) the dark mystery of sin entered into us. Whatever may be the source of that contagion, the door for its entry into the universe was and is our humanity. In that sense we are all Adam. In this way Paul expresses one half of this great thought. Now he opens the other massive door of hope and possibility. Just as through an event, an event now lost in the mists of time, evil entered human experience, so now, in an event very much within our history and knowledge, the very opposite happens. Grace, life, power, forgiveness — all these things flow into our humanity because of the entry of Jesus Christ into it and his assumption of all aspects of it.

> *Much more will those who receive the abundance of grace and the free gift of righteousness reign in life through the one man Jesus Christ*

Notice that Paul doesn't describe an ancient dualism which is to continue for ever between two equally matched forces. For Paul the consequence of Christ's role in history will be of infinitely greater power than that of Adam. In other words, Paul is setting out an immensely hopeful portrait of humanity.

Third Reading

In this passage of Matthew's Gospel, we listen to Our Lord telling his followers about the future. It is important to realize that, by the time Matthew is writing, that same future has arrived. Those who heard him are now finding themselves in situations which bring back Our

Lord's words and images. In much the same way we, in yet another and further future, have to ask what those words say to us about our situation as Christians in society.

> *A disciple is not above his teacher, nor a*
> *servant above his master*

The most creative and enabling attitude for anyone to adopt is to regard every person with whom one comes in contact as potentially one's teacher, and likewise to regard every person with whom one comes in contact as a person whom one may in some way serve.

> *They* [*will*] *malign those of his*
> *household*

Christians today need a certain realism about their situation. There are elements in society who are prepared not only to reject Christianity but to attack it in any way possible. Christian realism calls for an awareness of this fact without becoming paranoid about it. For instance, one area of contemporary life where Christianity must discover new ways to express and commend its point of view is the media.

> *Do not fear those who kill the body but*
> *cannot kill the soul*

Such a statement has a chilling and yet unreal ring for most Western Christians, particularly in North America. Until recently we were inclined to recall this kind of New Testament statement as an echo of a far-away and long-ago situation. Within the last half century, and even more particularly in the last couple of decades, that feeling of long-ago has vanished. In a number of societies, perhaps most notably in South Africa and in Central

America, there have been and still are martyrdoms, in the most literal and traditional meaning of that word. Men and women who have taken a public stand on issues of justice, basing their positions on the Christian gospel, have died for such positions in the belief that those who could kill their bodies could not kill their souls.

> *Even the hairs of your head are all*
> *numbered. Fear not, therefore*

Again there is that conviction which we came across in the Genesis passage above. Each human life is seen as being of significance to God. This conviction is acted upon with a great courage and nobility in the lives of many Soviet dissidents. In many cases their stands are taken on the basis of deep Christian faith, sometimes Russian Orthodox, sometimes Jewish. Their stances, often maintained in solitude of the most threatening kind, are taken on the conviction that the witness of one man or woman is of intense significance, precisely because each man and woman is of unique and eternal significance to God.

> *Everyone who acknowledges me before*
> *men*

One of the most important questions for what we have come to call mainline Christians is that of witnessing to their faith. If Christian faith is to have a future, it must be communicated. It must in some sense be evangelical. But what is acceptable and effective evangelism in a pluralistic society? This is a question for which we must find answers. Quite obviously, from any understanding of New Testament faith, it is not enough merely to acknowledge Jesus as Lord within oneself. There is a duty to communicate faith. The questions centre around how we are to do this. How is a man or woman to communicate effectively and acceptably what Our Lord Jesus Christ means in their life and in their thinking?

Psalm

Perhaps more than any other expression of faith in the Bible, these verses affirm a man or woman's personal significance as a creature of a loving God. We are beings who are "bound to God in love." Many images of life flicker for a moment in the sequence of verses. Life is obviously not preserved by passivity or self-protection in these images! All is activity, even risk. Life is lived passionately and richly, precisely because faith allows a higher degree of trust.

Sunday between 26 June and 2 July

Genesis 32:22–32
Romans 6:3–11
Matthew 10:34–42
Psalm 17:1–7, 16

Theme The struggle and the frequent cost of Christian faith. We first see the spiritual struggle in our own divided humanity as Jacob wrestles (Genesis). Paul then discusses the quest for renewal in us all and the ''dying'' which is the price paid (Romans). Finally we hear Our Lord telling us the unavoidable costs of our allegiance to his kingdom, as each of us understands it (Matthew).

First Reading

Jacob arose, sent everything [and everybody] he had across the stream, and was left alone

We are entering a long drama near a great and late scene. Jacob has spent his life dreading this inevitable encounter with the brother (Esau) whom he had wronged. He knows they must meet tomorrow. Jacob has surrounded himself with possessions. For Jacob even people are possessions to be used. He is alone. Being so can be very difficult. Few of us are good at being alone. We tend to avoid it.

A man wrestled with him

We know where Jacob was that night. The Jabbok is a small river in a steep-sided wadi. It enters the Jordan from the east. In Jacob's day it was a common belief that at night the spirit of the river took shape and could be encountered. All of us encounter spirits in the dark hours — spirits of fear, anxiety, regret, guilt. Like Jacob we can sometimes wrestle with them for hours and be exhausted next day. When the scripture speaks of a "man" wrestling with Jacob, it also expresses a profound reality which we today might express as Jacob's other self, his shadow or dark side, which we all possess.

Jacobs' thigh was put out of joint

Our wrestling is always costly in some way. The shadow side of our nature, because it knows us so well (after all it inhabits us), can explore and exploit our most vulnerable parts. It can wrench us psychologically and emotionally and, therefore, as we well know, have physical effects on us.

Jacob said, "I will not let you go, unless you bless me"

Jacob is being very wise. He knows, as we would be wise to know, that such wrestling can become a blessing to us. Facing fears, naming guilts, defining anxieties can be very healing.

Your name shall no more be called Jacob

In scripture there is always great significance in a name change. It expresses some great change in a person. We ask, What's in a name? The true answer is, A great deal. When inner wrestling becomes a healing process, it also becomes a changing process. It can change a personality. One level of meaning in "Jacob" becoming "Israel" is that Jacob, because of this searing experience, becomes a bigger person.

> *"Tell me"* [*said Jacob*] *"your name."*
> *But he said, "Why is it that you ask my*
> *name?"*

There is irony here for a reason already mentioned. Jacob does not have to be told the name of the other. The name of the other is Jacob, the other Jacob!

> *I have seen God face to face*

For a Christian this is a most important statement. For a Christian nothing is "just" psychological, a dream is not "just" a dream, a fear is not "just" a neurosis. All of these things are instruments of the dealings of a loving God with us.

> *The sun rose upon him as he passed,*
> *limping*

It is a beautiful metaphor of the human experience. We can be triumphant even though wounded.

Second Reading   *Baptized into Jesus Christ . . . baptized into his death*

The phrase is deliberately and powerfully paradoxical, particularly in our society where baptism is thought of as linked with birth, and death with old age. I think we can too easily assume that all understand this paradoxical link between baptism and death. Put simply, there is a great insight at the heart of human experience.

It is not specifically Christian. It is found in every culture in some form and expressed in some ritual way. It is that we must somehow die to come alive again renewed. In Christian experience baptism, particularly adult baptism, is the acting out of this great eternal truth.

> *We were buried with him by baptism*

There are two images mingled here. The image of the body of Jesus being placed in the tomb, and the image of ourselves being placed under water.

> *As Christ was raised . . . we too might walk in newness of life*

Again two powerful images are projected on our minds simultaneously. Christ is raised from the tomb; we emerge renewed from the baptismal waters. At that moment in our lives, or when we witness that moment, we are experiencing this immensely powerful truth on many levels. As we watch the person come from baptism, we know there has been spiritual renewal, but we know also that there will be many occasions in life when we will have to experience little deaths from which, by God's grace, we will emerge renewed.

> *If we have died with Christ we believe that we shall also live with him*

Paul is expressing a Christian hope which applies not only to the end of our physical existence. At all stages of our lives we are moving through the process of dying and living again. If we trust that the great and ultimate dying and rising of Our Lord is true, then that trust will enable us to move through the many lesser transitory deaths and rebirths in our experience.

Our old self was crucified with him

Again Christian faith is expressing the truth that if we offer our self-will ("old self") to Christ as he offered his self-will to the will of God, then we find a new self returned to us, whose will is in accord with Christ and regards him as its Lord.

Third Reading

We again meet the theme of struggle. We met it in Jacob's personal struggle and in the images used by Paul to express the struggle for renewal of our human nature. Now Jesus speaks of struggle in another sense.

> *I have not come to bring peace but a sword*

It is a hard and chilling statement of Our Lord. Those who try to present the gospel as lovely and gentle and sentimental find no help here. Conflict at some level and in some circumstances is unavoidable.

> *A man against his father, daughter against her mother. A man's foes will be those of his own household*

Christian allegiance is sometimes costly in terms of family relationships. Sometimes children disappoint parents by refusing Christian commitment. And sometimes parents whose faith has atrophied are not only amazed but also made guilty and angry at the flowering of a personally discovered faith by the new generation. In societies where social ferment and religious loyalties are intertwined — as in South and Central America and in some parts of Africa — families can find themselves torn apart politically when the understanding of Christian responsibility differs radically between the generations. This scripture is painfully contemporary.

> *He who loses his life for my sake will find it*

This is a profound truth which men and women have come to in many ways. It is related to Paul's telling us in the Epistle that to offer one's ''old self'' to Christ is to lose it but also to find one's real or true self.

> *Whoever gives to one of these little ones even a cup of cold water*

Another moment when the nature of Christian love is defined, not in terms of an abstract or cerebral spirituality but in terms of the concrete and the practical.

Psalm

A pleading song from one who longs for a good relationship with God. There is also an element here of something our society wrestles with in human terms, the longing for acceptance. The singer claims to have lived relatively blamelessly, claims integrity, purity, obedience to the law. Yet there is still the longing for God. As Augustine said, ''Our hearts are restless till they find their rest in thee.''

Sunday between 3 and 9 July

Exodus 1:6–14, 22—2:10
Romans 7:14–25a
Matthew 11:25–30
Psalm 124

Theme In all three readings and in the Psalm there is discernible a recurring image of God as in some sense an ally of our humanity. In the experience of Israel's struggle with the Egyptians and their risk-taking in the Red Sea, God is ally (Exodus). In the inner moral struggle of our humanity Christ offers himself as our ally (Romans). The voice of Our Lord invites us to accept his simplicity, his nearness to God, and his rule, thus to find our rest within (Matthew).

First Reading   *Joseph died and all his generation*

The storyteller wishes to bring an act of a great play or story to a close, thereby making it very obvious that the next great act is about to begin.

There arose a new king

It is easy to forget that this very phrase has had an ominous ring for Jewish minorities all over the world down the centuries. Always there is the question about the attitude of the present or a new regime to Jews. The statement is not merely an ancient biblical one.

> *Let us deal with them . . . set*
> *taskmasters. The more they were*
> *oppressed, the more they multipled. The*
> *Egyptians were in dread. They made*
> *(Israel) serve with rigour*

The scenario in those phrases is dismally familiar. There are societies on at least three continents to which this scenario is totally applicable today.

> *Every son . . . you shall cast into the*
> *Nile*

The situation now moves from economic oppression to selective genocide.

> *A man from the house of Levi took a*
> *wife*

We now begin a story full of ironies and many layers of meaning. In this story God will take the unexpected and use it creatively. The great river intended as a river of death will become a river of life. The Egyptians themselves, desperate to deprive Israel of a future, will become the very means of providing an instrument for that future. We look at the sequence.

> *She put the child in the basket made of*
> *bulrushes and placed it . . . at the*
> *river's brink*

The image is familiar in "the great code" of the Bible. Here again is the ship, the ark, which bears human life on the waters. Or here is a seed placed within the waters of the world's womb, trusting that the Lord of history will see that it is fertilized.

> *His sister stood at a distance . . . The*
> *daughter of Pharoah came. The child's*
> *mother took him.*

Notice how the child, the seed, the repository of the future is surrounded by the feminine. All of them together will make the future possible.

> *When she opened it she saw the child*

Pharoah's daughter will become for the early Christians centuries later a virginal figure, taking the child to herself. Moses and Jesus will blend as images, one becoming the forerunner of the other, each freeing a people and forming them into a new people.

> *She named him Moses "because I drew*
> *him out of the water"*

Layers of symbolism lie in this moment. The ark has once again grounded safely on Ararat, and the future begins. The child is taken to the arms of the princess and another future begins. Israel will come from the waters of the nearby Red Sea. A carpenter will come from the waters of the far-away Jordan. You and I will be lifted from the waters of baptism. The meanings are rich, many levelled, endless, and very powerful.

Second Reading   *The law is spiritual, but I am carnal*

We are now reading one of the greatest wrestlings with the human predicament ever done. We are confronting a gulf within human nature, within each one of us. One way to try to define that gulf is between what is and what we know should be, between actual and ideal, between what Paul would call spirit and flesh.

> *I can will what is right but I cannot do it*

We have all been there. One knows what is the right thing to do. One knows all the reasons why one should do it, yet one does not do it. One hates oneself for not doing it and still one does not do it! But our situation is even worse.

> *I do not do the good I want, but the evil I do not want is what I do.*

This is cause for even greater moral frustration and self-loathing. Something dark and strong laughs at all my efforts to will myself not to do something. And as it laughs it twists something in my deepest being and I do what I do not want to do. Notice, however, that we have just said "something dark and strong." We are reaching the same conclusion Paul reached when he said,

> *If I do what I do not want, it is no longer I that do it, but sin which dwells within me*

In other words, I have company within myself, another source of willing and wanting. I am occupied territory. I have, as Paul goes on to say, "another law at war with the law of my mind." We hardly need to explain it. We all experience it. This "other" is perfectly familiar to each of us. It is not for nothing that the medieval world, when it wanted to express the fact that it thought someone was the captive of evil, would say that he or she had "a familiar," and they would sometimes presume it embodied physically, usually as an animal.

> *Who will deliver us from this body of death?*

If my deepest self is fated to be perpetually at war with an enemy which twists my will at every turn, then I am immobilized. What other images are useful? Divided? Frustrated? Schizoid? The next thought is — if my will to good has an enemy within myself who is always on the side of the evil in me, then I must seek out and find an ally who will enter into my deepest self and be on the side of the good in me. This is the dramatic moment when Paul points me to Jesus Christ and tells me that there is my ally. Christ as Holy Spirit has offered to indwell me. My voice and Paul's say together,

> *Thanks be to God through Jesus Christ Our Lord!*

Third Reading

There is a note of quiet devotional reflection in this reading. Near to me as he is, what Our Lord has to tell me is essentially simple (not easy), and deeply healing.

> *Hidden from the wise, revealed to babes*

Here and elsewhere in the Gospels there is the reminder that the good news (and/or the kingdom) does not need great intelligence or philosophy or education to receive it. This does not mean that these things cannot receive it, merely that they are not necessary. What is necessary is to have within us, always being nourished and used, the "inner child" within our adulthood.

No one knows the Father except the Son

If I wish to comprehend in any way the ultimate mystery at the heart of creation then I look at, listen to, and allow myself to be touched by Jesus Christ.

You will find rest for your souls

Jesus offers himself to me as an ultimate focus of my life's longing and searching. This truth can be expressed and has been in endless images. He is the ultimate bread I hunger for, the ultimate relationship I seek. He is the city I search for. A little silent reflection will give each of us the image which for us expresses this deep and lovely truth at the heart of the gospel.

Psalm

In the opening and ending phrase is the central song in this passage. It echoes the single thread which runs through all three scriptures — the idea of God being with us as ally in our struggles.

Sunday between 10 and 16 July

Exodus 2:11–22
Romans 8:9–17
Matthew 13:1–9,
18–23
Psalm 69:6–15

Theme In the three readings we see three processes by which something new and good emerges from God's purposes. The real hidden Moses begins to emerge from behind the false persona (Exodus). Our real self begins to emerge as we grow spiritually from self-centredness (flesh) to the Spirit of Christ (Romans). In Our Lord's parable the seed struggles to emerge everywhere and eventually finds good ground (Matthew).

First Reading   *One day, when Moses had grown up*

As we well know, "growing up" does not happen on a particular day. It is a gradual and, for the most part, unconscious process. And yet there can also be moments when it does flood into our consciousness, or perhaps shows other people around us that we have "grown up," unknown to ourselves until this particular moment.

He went out to his people and looked on their burdens

Already in Moses an identification has taken place. We don't know if this is conscious (did the royal house tell him of his origins?) or not. But the writer makes it obvious in subtle ways that Moses feels drawn to these ("his") people and has become sensitive to their "burdens." A very valid modern parallel is the inner turmoil which drew Mahatma Ghandi back to India and its untouchables from being a relatively successful South African lawyer.

He [Moses] killed the Egyptian

It sounds a sudden impulsive act, a focusing of a depth of inner revulsion he himself has not fully been aware of until this moment. Very often, at lesser levels than this, a sudden action done or word said can shock us into realizing unsuspected depths of feeling about something.

And hid him in the sand

The impulsive nature of the killing is made obvious by Moses' reaction. Not only must the body be dug into the sand, but the thoughts, the feelings, the act must be put back into the unconscious from which they have burst. But, of course, we cannot ever completely do that.

Who made you a prince and judge? Do you mean to kill me?

It's too late to put the demon back into the bottle. Everything has utterly changed. What the unknown and courageous Hebrew points out to Moses is the reality he himself doesn't yet realize. The royal prince is irrevocably gone. Moses has stepped for ever out of a charmed circle. Sometimes we refuse to acknowledge certain realities which we have brought about by things said or done. It takes someone else to make us recognize reality, and sometimes this needs to be done harshly.

Pharoah sought to kill Moses

Sometimes we come to realize that the harsh collision with reality which someone else has forced us to recognize was not harsh at all. It may well have prevented something far worse happening. The Hebrew slave's brutal dismissal of the authority Moses is still trying to cling to actually saves his life. A chapter of life ends, suddenly, before it is realized. Many of us know such sudden and unexpected changes.

Moses sat down by a well

There is in the telling a hint of a new Moses. This is a human being whose world has fallen apart. There needs to be reflection. Is the well an image of the grace Moses needs and will in time receive? What "wells" do we often come by without realizing their potential grace?

Shepherds drove [the women] away, but Moses helped them

Once again an insight into Moses' character. This is the second time he has stood with the weak and the oppressed.

Moses was content to dwell . . . he gave Moses his daughter . . . she bore a son

Moses has changed. A chapter seems over for ever. Yet no chapter of one's life is ever over. The past can become preparation for the future. We can meet our past in our future sometimes in a way which allows much to be achieved.

Second Reading   *You are not in the flesh, you are in the Spirit, if in fact the Spirit of God dwells in you*

Remember that "flesh" does not mean merely the physical. It means paradoxically a rival spirit to the spirit of God. We might say the spirit of self.

Anyone who does not have the Spirit of Christ

Not to "have the Spirit of Christ" is not to have handed over our "self" to his rule. In every-day life that might mean quite literally asking a total real Christ in our lives, "What do you want me to do in this situation?" To have that "other" in one's life is a great part of what being a Christian, man or woman, means.

If Christ is in you . . . your spirits are alive

A universally true experience of those who have consciously committed themselves to Jesus Christ as Lord. There is a sense of being more vibrantly alive.

Because of righteousness

The ghastly nuances we have given to that great word righteousness make it sound as if Christians are insufferably self-righteous! Yet all that Paul is say-ing is that Christians can be alive with the knowledge not that they have somehow made themselves "right" with God, but that quite undeservedly God has set things "right" between himself and them!

> *He who raised Jesus Christ from the*
> *dead will give life to your mortal bodies*

Of course, the scripture is speaking of the mystery that somehow physical elements take part in the process of resurrection. But something else is true, that to be a spiritual man or woman can exert a therapeutic or healing influence on us physically.

> *All who are led by the Spirit of God are*
> *sons of God . . . not the spirit of slavery*
> *. . . we are children of God . . . if*
> *children then heirs*

I have quoted all these phrases because together they are a great echoing cry of Paul to get us to grasp a magnificent truth. The relationship between God and those who seek God in Jesus Christ is one of parent and child, with all the intimacy and ease which that suggests! That concept contradicted all the surrounding views of divinity in the empire of Paul's time. In our own time it remains unrealized by all too many.

> *Provided we suffer with him in order*
> *that we may also be glorified with him*

There is a kick in the end of this scripture. The relationship with Our Lord is with one who suffered. Our relationship with him must come at some cost if it is to be real.

Third Reading   *He got into a boat . . . and told them many things*

An immediate image of the intimacy Jesus himself set out to model, an intimacy between God and our humanity. As Jesus uses the boat which is so integral to their lives, so God uses the normal fabric of human life, communicating through it and present within it.

A sower went out to sow

With these words begins one of the most vivid of all Our Lord's parables. It is also the only parable to which an explanation or commentary is added.

When anyone hears the word of God and does not understand

In every one of the situations outlined by Our Lord in the parable, the important step is what happens after the good news of the kingdom is heard in a person's life. Hearing it is never enough. The question is what our response is going to be. The first essential is to understand it. Understanding can mean effort, an investment of one's time in such things as study and prayer, preferably though not necessarily with others.

Receives the word with joy . . . when tribulation arises . . . immediately falls away

To hear Our Lord say this is salutary because none of us knows how resilient our faith will be in the face of real trouble. We may already have come through such a time of personal suffering or professional stress or even bereavement. We may already have discovered that our faith became a very real resource in the circumstance. If so, we give thanks.

> *Cares of the world and delight in riches choke the word*

What Our Lord may be referring to in terms of today's world is the whole frantic involvement of our lives. This need not mean an involvement in evil things. Our busy-ness may well be quite vacuous and harmless! "Riches" need not mean financial wealth so much as the overrich mixture of choices we have available to us to occupy time, consume energy, titillate appetites. In such fashion life becomes filled, and the illusion arises that life on such terms is its own meaning.

> *Good soil . . . hears . . . understands . . . bears fruit*

The quality of Christian faith very succinctly defined. It is heard. But then the hearer invests something of him or herself to achieve a deeper understanding, a clearer vision. Then comes the stage of growth which makes all the difference.

Psalm

Obviously the writer is experiencing a most difficult period. Whatever has happened has alienated even his or her family. Whether real or imagined (for we often imagine social rejection if we are tired or depressed) he or she feels a laughing stock. Yet we hear three very fine things. The writer readily acknowledges "foolishness" and "fault." He or she is concerned about the effect of mistakes on others. And finally we hear an undiminished trust that God will help.

Sunday between 17 and 23 July

Exodus 3:1–12
Romans 8:18–25
Matthew 13:24–30,
36–43
Psalm 103:1–13

Theme All three readings are expressions of God's involvement in history. In the Exodus passage God's determination to offer liberation to an oppressed people. In the Romans passage we are given Paul's dream of liberation being offered to the totality of creation. In the Gospel passage we are shown human history, always flawed by moral ambiguity yet awaiting a total evaluation or judgement by God — a liberation from evil.

First Reading   *Moses was keeping the flock*

From royal sophisticate to desert farmer. The two are worlds apart. Perhaps that is the way it has to be if real change is to be brought about. For a while there is for Moses that strange gift we often don't want but badly need, the gift of solitude. It's the gift we regularly refuse because we are not sure we wish to be alone with ourselves. And is it only with ourselves? Is there another to be encountered? We hesitate to place ourselves where that encounter may take place?

*Moses came to Horeb, the mountain of
God*

There are no signs on such moun-
tains in our lives, labelling them neatly as dwelling places
of God. We have to discover that, sometimes in strange
ways, and sometimes, sadly, we pass by not recognizing
a "Horeb."

*The angel of the Lord appeared in a
flame of fire out of the midst of a bush*

Many bushes burn in our everyday
lives. One day there comes such a fire which is more than
the everyday. We are perhaps in a certain mood. We have
certain needs. We are for a while vulnerable. At such a
moment the ordinary becomes more. An angel comes. We
are communicated with.

Moses said, "I will turn aside"

The former Moses might not have.
There would have been distraction, a royal reception to
reach on time, a temple rite to be performed. The chariot
might have been going too fast! But this new Moses has
time. His world is going slower. Sometimes it is only when
we are prepared to go slower that we notice a light beyond
the ordinary.

*When the Lord saw that he turned aside
to see, God called to him*

It is not usually God's way to force
our attention. If we open the door, God comes in to sup
with us. The door is rarely pushed in. Sometimes it is. It
was so with Saul who would become Paul. But rarely is it so.

Moses said, "Here I am"

Is there a hint that Moses knows at last "where he is" inside himself, that precisely because of this he can now become a valuable instrument for a will other than his own. He has been broken and put back together again.

The place you are standing is holy ground

A sentence for all of us. It reminds us that the processes and experiences we label (quite rightly) as psychological are for a Christian not just psychological. We have not just encountered a part of ourselves. We have in that encounter met another. The moment and the place are holy.

I am the God of your father, the God of Abraham, Isaac, and Jacob

All of the past is part of the present. The present moment isn't isolated, having its own detached meaning. It grows out of the past and has deep roots which can, if we grasp them, give us strength.

Moses hid his face, for he was afraid to look at God

We do well to be afraid at moments of encounter because they come for a purpose, a purpose other than and higher than ours. We may expect consequences, a task, a vocation. Our fear is well founded. The task may be the one we have always dreaded because it involves the past, and the past can be painful. So it was with Moses. God said, "I will send you to Pharoah."

> *Moses said, "Who am I that I should go to Pharoah"*

An ironic reply. He is the very person to go. He speaks the language. He knows the area. He knows how the Egyptian mind thinks. All his past has prepared him, but he doesn't realize it. Why? Because he doesn't want to. Often we don't realize our potential because to do so would be too daunting. It would ask too much of us. Fear of our own potential can, ironically, immobilize us.

> *God said, "I will be with you"*

Five deceptively simple words, so simple that we frequently do not discern the enormous promise they contain in all our lives.

Second Reading
In this passage Paul, in a vast sweep of insight, anticipates the glory already seen in Our Lord eventually being experienced by the totality of creation. But it is also possible to choose to homilize on this passage in terms of personal experience.

> *The glory that is to be revealed*

We saw in Moses a tendancy to presume that, after leaving his Egyptian chapter of life behind, the significant part of his life was over. That can be a common self-deception. The degree to which we can anticipate new challenges, the degree to which we can think in terms of more "to be revealed" for us, is the measure of a healthy attitude to life.

Creation was subjected to futility

Paul describes a universal human experience. A sense of futility sweeps over us all at some time or other. In fact it can attack at times of our seeming successes.

Set free from the bondage of decay . . . obtain the glorious liberty of the children of God

Paul is getting at something very profound. While a sense of futility about life can be deeply troubling and can, if not challenged, destroy us, nevertheless Paul is suggesting that this same futility can be a healthy reminder that no purpose and no cause in our lives can give absolute fulfilment (it in some sense "decays"). The only absolutely satisfying and liberating human experience is God! The presence of God, the glory of God, the love of God, the peace of God. It remains no less a mystery after all our groping language, but there are moments when we know this to be not merely a reality but reality itself!

We groan inwardly as we wait . . . in this hope we are saved

We are embodied beings. That is not said to denigrate our bodies. We are not prisoners in our bodies and therefore cut off from God. Rather our total self — body, mind, and spirit — is not yet whole. There is in our human condition a "not yet." There is more, to use C.S. Lewis's phrase. That "more," that "not yet," is what we hope for, and we are given glimpses of it in ways we sometimes hesitate to communicate even to those nearest to us.

Third Reading *A man sowed good seeds . . . his enemy*
sowed weeds . . . the weeds are the sons
of the evil one . . . the enemy is the
devil

I gathered these phrases together to
emphasize that Our Lord's view of evil is not to regard it
as merely the absence of good. For Our Lord evil is a reality
— active, purposeful, formidable.

Good seed in his field . . . weeds among
the wheat

The field is life as we know it. It is
human affairs, human history, human experience. In it all
there is a mixture of values present. Always and in
everything — in every act, every intention, every motive,
every process — there is moral ambiguity.

Do you want us to gather [the weeds]?
Let both grow together until the harvest

There is something of a paradox here.
It is a reflection of the complexity of our human condition.
It is not that we are to ignore the weeds (the elements of
evil) in all human beings. We are supposed to be very aware
of them but not to have the illusion that our judgement is
so clear that we can always tell "weed" from "wheat." The
sad fact is that our very judgement is itself damaged by "the
enemy."

Let both grow together until the harvest

There is a sense in which we have no
choice! We must. In other words, all human effort and

thought and action is going to have "weeds and wheat" together in it. Our Lord is saying that the whole human story is lived within a context or a history which involves a final evaluation or judgement. Therefore, in every decision and action we are always responsible and accountable.

Psalm

A portrait of God as gentle, forgiving, and merciful. The Psalm echoes the theme of the Exodus passage and of the Gospel. In his awareness of the plight of an enslaved people, God's care is shown. In God's "executing of righteousness and judgement" we glimpse the same inevitability of a reckoning which Our Lord speaks of in the Gospel message.

Sunday between 24 and 30 July

Exodus 3:13–20
Romans 8:26–30
Matthew 13:44–52
Psalm 105:1–11

Theme There is a "searching" theme all through these scriptures. Moses is searching to grasp what God wants him to do, searching for the resolve to do it (Exodus). Our inabilities to pray, even to believe, drive us to a search for grace. The very urge to search is itself evidence of the presence of a Spirit (Romans). Searching for the hidden kingdom of heaven among our lived experiences is what the life of faith is about (Matthew).

First Reading   *Moses said to God, "If I come*

All through this scripture Moses is dragging his heels, testing the waters, probing the reality of the situation. It is too facile to dismiss the process of this scripture as expressing Moses' fears or his unwillingness to accept a vocation readily and without hesitation. It is this very carefulness which will make him a good leader in the future.

If they ask me, "What is his name?"

Moses has vivid and searing memories of his first and last attempt to help the Hebrew situation.

Oppressed people are wisely suspicious of highly placed idealists who come with ringing calls to action!

> *God said, "Say this, 'I AM has sent me to you' "*

Tell them, says God, that an ultimate reality, more real than their slavery, more real than their present sense of defeat, more real than anything they are aware of, has now come to them. That is how revolutions happen. A reality, more real than all the factors creating oppression, comes. It comes as conviction, as vision, as solidarity. It comes as that which is! It is for those people that which names itself "I AM."

> *God also said, "Say this, 'The Lord, the God of your fathers, has sent me to you' "*

A recapturing of identity, a regaining of their own history, can give people a sense of who they are. Regaining memory of their past can recreate a hope for the future.

> *I will bring you up out of affliction to the land of the Canaanites, the Hittites . . . a land flowing with milk and honey*

Notice the realism. There is not a promise to move from affliction to milk and honey. Between the two is the real cost and sacrifice. The land will have to be earned, struggled for, achieved. Sacrifices will have to be made. It is the pattern of human existence. The only easy way from "Egypt" to "the land of milk and honey" is the lottery ticket! Even then there is the possibility of getting lost in a self-created wilderness!

The king of Egypt will not let you go
unless compelled by a mighty hand

Again realism. Great things are not done merely by fervent religious posturing. They are done through human commitment, the bringing to bear of human insights, human gifts, human power, none of which are evil unless they are totally self-centred and focused only on the achievement of power. Offered to a vision beyond themselves or offered to a bond beyond themselves, they become the stuff which God uses to form history.

Second Reading *The Spirit helps us in our weakness*

Notice how this simple statement describes what we have seen take place with Moses in the previous reading! There are times when we feel totally inadequate. At such times we possess a source of grace if we turn to it. Notice too how we are being told that it is in our periods of weakness and felt inadequacy that the Spirit is most available to us.

We do not know how to pray as we
ought

Very few do! There are those who have worked hard and long at prayer. For most of us prayer is a jumbled and tattered effort. There are many different kinds of prayer — praise, thanksgiving, confession, adoration — but for the most part we enter into different modes of prayer perhaps for a moment and for a very specific reason. Such prayer is not to be sneered at. Even a moment of prayer is significant. God is not a counter of seconds or minutes or hours.

> *The Spirit himself intercedes for us with signs too deep for words*

First, this is a reminder that prayer is not merely words and specific formed prayers. To realize our life is lived always in the presence of God, in the love of Jesus Christ, and in the company of the Holy Spirit within us — that is to have an attitude of prayer even if words and formed prayers are not being said. Secondly, when we cannot pray because there is a deep shadow across our lives, whether it be pain or sorrow or loss of faith or whatever, it can be immensely engracing to know that there is within us that unquenchable flame of the Holy Spirit who offers the cry for help which our conscious will cannot.

> *He who searches the hearts of men knows what is the mind of the Spirit*

The searcher being referred to is of course the Lord, but I think it helpful to mention something this scripture also points to. Those men and women who search the human heart — spiritual directors, counsellors, psychiatrists — realize, if their work is done in a context of Christian faith, that the work of the Holy Spirit goes on not only in our conscious minds but in all the layers of subconscious and unconscious. As Paul says next, "in everything" at all levels of our lives, "God works for good."

> *God works for good with those who love him*

Christian life is a dialogue between the soul and God. It is not a divine monologue of orders and exhortations, nor a human monologue of requests and petitions and expressions of guilt. We are the raw material through whom God works, but that can only be if we offer ourselves for the working.

Third Reading   *The kingdom of heaven*

Whenever Our Lord uses this phrase, he is communicating images of reality as it exists under the rule and will of God. It is as if Our Lord is saying, "If human life and God's life could be together completely, human life totally reflecting God's will for us, then this is how things would be, this is what would happen."

Like treasure hidden

First of all, it is of immense value to possess a sense of "the kingdom," of knowing that one is the child of such a kingdom, living in a kind of exile from it, discovering glimpses of it from time to time. Those glimpses come if we realize that the kingdom is not another place or another time but is "hidden" among the experiences through which we move.

Sells all that he has and buys that field

How much is Christian faith worth to us? How much is a sense of the presence of God, of the love of Christ, of the peace and meaning that such realities can bring into one's life? How much are these things worth? Each of us makes that decision in many ways. The ultimate truth (the "kingdom of heaven" truth) is that these realities are worth everything! Where do we stand on that scale of valuing our relationship with Our Lord?

A net [which] gathered fish of every kind

An image of the kingdom which introduces a stern note. The kingdom is certainly a state of joy, but there is also warning. The joy is achieved by our response and commitment. When we offer ourselves (our thinking, our gifts, our loyalties) to Our Lord we find a deep sense of meaning and satisfaction (joy) in our ongoing life. But there are many motivations among us all as we search in our different ways for the kingdom of heaven. Always we are accountable for our lives.

There are a number of ways we can apply this image of the net. The church itself is such a net. Its community contains a total spectrum of human motivations and intentions from the most self-centred to the most self-sacrificing. All are brought into the net. All are called to a process of change and growth in Christ. The first disciples were such a net with a very varied catch! We ourselves in the changing feelings and circumstances of our lives are at turns faithful and yet withdrawing from faith, enthusiastic yet resentful, giving yet withholding, loyal yet disloyal.

> *Threw away the bad . . . at the close of the age*

Not till then is the separation made. All of us are accepted at the level at which we offer ourselves. All of us are responsible for the quality of our commitment. The invitation always continues to be extended to come farther, to commit more deeply. Whatever degree to which we respond is accepted. Evaluation or judgement comes only when God brings the human story to the end that God alone intends and forms.

Psalm

A song about the concept of *covenant*. To say that lovely word is to celebrate that humanity matters to God. To believe this in the late twentieth century is to find cause for joy. Constantly we should search out the ways of God in contemporary history. Above all we need to realize that, just as ancient Israel was given a land for which they were responsible, so contemporary humanity is given a planet for which we are responsible.

Sunday between 31 July and 6 August

Exodus 12:1–14
Romans 8:31–39
Matthew 14:13–21
Psalm 143:1–10

Theme The theme through all three scriptures is that our humanity is not sufficient itself. We need resources, grace, nourishment, from God. This is expressed in the very tangible symbols of the Passover meal (Exodus), in Paul's lyrical affirmation of the inseparable love of Christ for us (Romans), and in the use of bread and fishes by Our Lord to point to the availability of his grace for us.

First Reading
This month shall be for you the beginning of months

They are still very far from being a free people, but the process is beginning. Now they take as the first step the formation of their own symbols. The first of those symbols is to have their own calendar. To possess one's own significant times is to possess a history, a memory. When people begin to move toward freedom, they begin to define their own significant dates and celebrations. We see this happening across the world in the formation of various emerging nations.

> *On the tenth day they shall take every*
> *man a lamb . . . on the fourteenth day*
> *the whole assembly of Israel shall kill*
> *their lambs*

Again we notice how identity is brought back to a people who have lost it. They reach for symbols and rites which give them identity. The process is being acted out in this century with native peoples in North America, Africa, Australia, South America.

> *They shall eat the flesh that night*
> *roasted . . . unleavened bread . . . bitter*
> *herbs*

The instructions are almost obsessively precise. Why? Because achieving utmost conformity even in this symbolic action creates deep social solidarity.

> *Your loins girded, your sandals on your*
> *feet, your staff in your hand*

Why? Because immediately the meal is eaten, the journey into the future begins. The meal is preparation for real and very challenging involvement. The domesticity and peace and celebration of this meal is going to be rudely shattered by a people tearing themselves away with great agony from the oppressor society. Already as they eat, they can see the marks of the lamb's blood that they have daubed on the door frame. It reminds them that the price of the freedom they are going to seek is the spilling of blood.

Far away in the future there will be another meal which will become significant for another newly formed people. It will have another name, in fact it will have many names as it spreads across the world and down through the centuries. It too will have as its food a lamb, but it will be a symbolic lamb, a human life whose purity and self-sacrifice will bring to mind the timeless lamb of Passover. That meal will also have a sacred bread, because the one sacrificed has said that he is giving himself to be nourishing bread for his people, just as he sees himself giving his blood to be nourishing wine for them.

Eat it, your loins girded

That whole stance — having the meal only when fully prepared to set out — is being recaptured in the eucharist today as many stand to receive bread and wine. Another factor which returns us to this stance is the way contemporary eucharist hears a dismissal — "Go in peace to love and serve the Lord" — almost immediately after receiving bread and wine. The implication behind these changes is that the meal is given to strengthen and nourish us for activity in our daily life. We eat, drink, and go! Far from being innovations, these so-called changes link us back across the centuries to those men and women standing in the ghetto houses of ancient Egypt, waiting for the sun to set on the ending of their captivity.

Second Reading   *If God is for us, who is against us . . . it is God who justifies*

Again we can refer to contemporary history. In so many cultures where there is a new vision of social life, there is the passionate conviction that "God is for us." On a personal basis this scripture is reminding us that God affirms our total humanity even though it is flawed. God is not merely detached creator. God is not angry judge. Humanity has not become the enemy of God (there are voices who seem to come very near to saying this). God knows, our humanity must test God's affirmation of us but it continues.

> *Christ Jesus who died . . . who was*
> *raised . . . who is at the right hand of*
> *God . . . who intercedes for us*

Again Paul is giving us reason to be sure that our humanity is affirmed by God. In Our Lord our humanity has actually been assumed by God. By Our Lord it has actually been taken into God. In a most vivid image Paul shows us our own humanity in Our Lord as actually praying for us before God. We are not creatures standing on the other side of a great gulf from the city of the presence of God. But in Jesus part of our humanity has crossed the gulf, has been admitted to the city and represents us there!

> *Who shall separate us from the love of*
> *Christ?*

Here we have the poet in Paul emerging, as it does somewhere in almost every epistle. The list of troubles seems at first sight rather outside the experience of the average Christian in the West. It's important to realize that this list — "famine, nakedness, peril, sword" — is a very familiar experience for millions who are Christian in the Third World. There are socieities in ferment where Christians, both clergy and lay, can say with utmost literalness, "For thy sake we are being killed all the day long." Yet these very same people can feel themselves to be "more than conquerors through him who loved us."

Third Reading   *Jesus withdrew*

How often do we withdraw? We are not referring to a hastily taken holiday, as frantic and exhausting as the ongoing demands of our work, only in a different way. We are referring to the kind of withdrawal that is hinted at in the words "a lonely place apart." "Lonely" for us today has negative echoes. It need not be so. We are thinking about a place where we can be alone. Another word in the Gospel is *apart* — apart from others, apart from demands, responsibilities, deadlines. Of course being "alone" and "apart" are also threatening possibilities. We very often either consciously or unconsciously take steps to avoid being alone or apart, because in real aloneness and apartness we meet ourselves, and that is not the easiest of encounters!

> *When the crowds heard it, they followed*

We could use this image of crowds following Our Lord to tell us something else about our efforts to be truly alone. "Crowds" will always try to follow, invisible intangible "crowds" of responsibilities, plans, worries, uncompleted agenda of every sort. How should we try to deal with them? How did Our Lord?

> *He had compassion on them, and healed their sick*

Perhaps this scripture can be heard to say that we would be wise to have a receiving rather than rejecting attitude to all the incomplete nagging agenda which trail our effort to get apart. If we accept the legitimacy of the guilts and dissatisfactions, the sense of things done and undone, then that accepting of them as present and real, that compassion toward them, gives us some chance of seeing some healing take place. Matthew also says that Jesus

> *healed their sick*

Facing the particular agenda which dogs our efforts to be alone also enables us to do some evaluating of its content, seeing perhaps for the first time what is sick and healthy in it, unreal and real, neurotic or legitimate.

> *The disciples said, "Send the crowds away"*

We are still using "crowds" as an image of the interior crowding that thwarts apartness. Trying merely to "send them away," to pretend they have not come, simply doesn't work. We cannot send them away because in a real sense we have brought them!

> *Jesus said, "They need not go away; you give them something to eat"*

Our Lord might be heard saying to us, "Your inner 'crowds' do not have to be sent away, banished from your conscious only to go down into your unconscious. Instead you face them, talk to them, give yourself to them. You acknowledge them, you 'give them something' of yourself."

> *Taking the five loaves and the two fish . . . he blessed and broke and gave . . . and they all ate and were satisfied*

We feel sometimes that we have very limited resources to deal with our inner crowds, our inner demands. Yet if we offer those resources and at the same time, in even a moment of prayer, engage the resources of grace available to us, then we can deal in a "satisfying" way with the situation.

Psalm

The overriding image is that of a resolute and formidable "enemy" which we are simply not capable of dealing with on our own. The language is vivid and strong. The enemy "crushes" one and brings inner "darkness." One's "spirit faints." One tastes the horror of a great "pit." All of these images are applicable to the times of our inner darknesses. The great healing message of this Psalm is its assumption that God is other than available and our unfailing resource.

Sunday between 7 and 13 August

Exodus 14:19–31
Romans 9:1–5
Matthew 14:22–33
Psalm 106:4–12

Theme There is a connecting theme of divine grace being greater than limited human response. Israel, poised on the edge of destruction, is given a way to the future in spite of their own doubts (Exodus). Paul agonizes over the failure of Israel to accept Jesus as the Christ but also acknowledges the immense spiritual treasure Israel possesses (Romans). Peter, deperately trying to respond at an ultimate level of faith, has to acknowledge his human limits and so finds his humanity accepted and helped (Matthew).

First Reading   *The angel of God . . . the pillar of cloud . . . the pillar of fire*

It is now regarded as highly likely that the area in which these events took place about thirty-three centuries ago was in some way volcanically active. The point here is not whether this was so, but what effect such mani-festations had on the thinking of Israel. They saw these events not as a modern observer would, in a totally detached, scientific way. For Israel the events were signs of something else. Like all nature they were instruments of the Lord of nature. God was at work, and in this case, at work on their side! Thinking like this is foreign to our minds. We can speak of it only as memory. But scripture is claiming to be more than memory. It claims to be a timeless word of God. So we are forced to probe this passage for its meaning for us.

Because we do not think of God as intervening in the process of history, we find it difficult to think of God as at all involved in the formation of nations. We feel also that to think of God as directly involved ("the Lord fights for them"; "the Lord drove the sea back") is to claim arrogantly some kind of "manifest destiny," an attitude we have seen in this century to lead to some dark and terrible things. However, we are committed as Christians to the activity of the Holy Spirit in every realm of human life! We pray for our nation and its institutions. So we are committed to searching for those events and developments in our national life which for us can become "the angel of God, the pillar of fire, the pillar of cloud." What were those moments when we were guided for good or preserved from harm? When were we given leadership which led us through wilderness? These are valid categories for contemporary Christian thinking.

> *The people of Israel went into the sea on dry ground*

We have become so used to the story as a religious myth or as ancient history that we forget the courage needed to do this seemingly obvious act! The truth here for us is that it is not enough in life that opportunities be presented. There also has to be the courage to risk availing ourselves of the opportunities!

Israel saw the great work of the Lord

We do not find the significance of the event by trying to analyse (a very Western and modern attitude) what actually happened. The power and the meaning is what the participants saw in the event and the effect it had on their thinking. For Israel the passage through the Red Sea was a never-to-be-forgotten experience. A whole people saw it as their time of birth — coming from the waters. History for them began.

To notice an irony. There is, so far as we know, no mention of this event in Egyptian history. Who knows, in the affairs of an empire, it may have been an incident. On the other hand, perhaps the Egyptians had the wisdom to realize that it is rather healthy psychologically to minimize one's losses and maximize one's gains. Perhaps as Israel wisely did one, Egypt wisely did the other!

The people walked on dry ground
through the sea

This last image sums up an event which has had repercussions far beyond itself. The "Exodus" event, as we call it, is a pattern repeated in different ways by other people seeking freedom. They have experienced events which they saw as their "Moses" (leader), their "Egypt" (oppression), their "Red Sea" (risks taken for freedom), their "wilderness" (confused period). Mao Tse Tung would see history in these terms (without God!). In our own lives this same pattern is the map of our own growth and development and journeying.

Second Reading   *I am speaking the truth in Christ*

We are at a point of transition in this great letter of Paul. For the last three chapters he has been doing his best (a formidable best!) to find language for the new life we can find from knowing Jesus Christ. Paul's effort to do this is made even more intense because he is trying to communicate a personal experience. Now, as he tries to put others in touch with that experience, he feels the frustration that all of us have known when we try to communicate a personally shattering and wonderful experience. We have often assured a listener by such phrases as ''I really am telling you exactly what it is like'' or ''I swear I am not exaggerating!'' We, as is Paul, are appealing to be believed.

> *I have great sorrow . . . in my heart*

But Paul is also asking for his listeners' belief about something else. Paul is about to share the central agony of his life. We could say it was a disappointment and a frustration, but those words are not strong enough. The agony was the course of conduct which bitter experience had, he felt, forced him into. His great hope was to take the tremendous new reality he had found in Christ to his own people. So far that had resulted for the most part in failure.

> *I could wish that I were . . . cut off*
> *from Christ for the sake of . . . my*
> *kinsmen by race*

I would give anything, Paul is saying, to change this situation. Paul would not have been human not to ask himself sometimes if he himself was partly to blame for this failure. All of us do this in the face of something that is obviously not working out.

> *Sonship, the glory, the covenants . . .*
> *the giving of the law . . . of their race*
> *according to the flesh, is the Christ*

In talking about Israelites, of whom Paul is one, Paul is already using the words "they" and "theirs." Already he is distancing himself consciously, or unconsciously. But in these two verses (4 and 5) he also communicates so much about his love and admiration for his own people. A great longing goes through this recital of all that Judaism means. These two verses are just as true today of a living Judaism as they have ever been. If it was true in the past that Judaism exists in particular covenant with God and in particular relationship (sonship), then it is true today, and that very fact must govern our attitude to Judaism.

Third Reading   *[Jesus] dismissed the crowds . . . made the disciples go before him . . . went up on the mountain by himself to pray*

Put in that sequence the scene is vivid and very significant. This is the kind of rhythm we see in Jesus' life frequently. There will be great activity. He will be surrounded by people, all in some way claiming some part of his attention and energy. Then at a certain point, gently but firmly, Our Lord will bring all that to an end. The crowd will be dispersed; even the disciples move from him at his suggestion. There is no hint of curt dismissal, of hurt feelings. The time has come for a period of solitariness and prayer, solitariness to encounter his own being, prayer to reach out to the Father. We need to reflect on that, as we watch Our Lord, and ask ourselves if there is any such pattern in our own lives.

In the fourth watch . . . he came to them, walking on the sea

The last thing is to cheapen this magnificent moment of the Gospel by arguing about how it could happen. The point is that these are the terms in which it remained an unforgettable memory for the disciples. Why? Because it was precisely in the midst of their struggle that he came to them, not at high summer noon with the lake glistening and smooth and allowing them rest. And that is precisely how Christ can come to us within the times of our struggling.

> *Peter . . . bid me come to you on the water*

There are times when we have to pray, "Lord give me the ability to reach out for you, even though I have nothing to support me but my own doubting faith." As with Peter, that prayer is responded to by the invitation, "Come."

> *Peter got out of the boat and walked on the water . . . he saw the wind . . . beginning to sink he cried out*

We have all been there on those waves making our effort to reach out, walking on the water of our fragile would-be faith. Life is capable of producing some very strong and daunting winds and some formidable waves. When we feel we are going under, we are in good company. Greater men and women than we have had to acknowledge total helplessness.

> *Peter cried out, "Lord save me." Jesus . . . caught him*

The important thing is the admission of need, the acknowledgement of not being in charge. The very admission opens the gates for others to respond, and opens the gates within us to accept their help.

Psalm

The psalm begins very personally (vv 4 and vv 5). The writer realizes that God has taken a hand in their history as a nation. The plea now is for the presence and help of God in personal experience. That is a very human and very understandable prayer which we need never hesitate to make. The rest of the psalm (vv 6-12) is a celebration of the fact that God's giving of grace and help does not depend on our human response. God's generosity is greater than human infidelity.

Sunday between 14 and 20 August

Exodus 16:2–15
Romans 11:13–16,
29–32
Matthew 15:21–28
Psalm 78:1–3, 10–20

Theme Receiving the grace of God and possessing a relationship with God is not dependant on our fragile capacity to remain faithful. Grace and relationship continue to be offered. We see this in the tensions and confrontations of a people in the wilderness (Exodus). We read of the longing of God to offer mercy and acceptance to all humanity (Romans). We see Our Lord called beyond the limits of his own humanity to embody that universal compassion in his ministry (Matthew).

First Reading

The people of Israel came to the wilderness

Everybody does come to the wilderness as they make the human journey. It is not a pleasant experience. One has things in reasonable control and plans are fairly well formed. Then suddenly nothing is under control, and plans are no longer possible because the conditions have all changed. Suddenly there are far more questions than answers, and the neat answers one had no longer apply. That is wilderness.

> *Israel murmured against Moses and
> Aaron in the wilderness*

Very often the effect of finding oneself in the wilderness is to look for a reason. After all, this is not one's normal, well-planned, organized existence! Something must not only be the reason, somebody must be to blame. Sometimes, of course, oneself is to blame, but not always. Getting into some wilderness situations is unavoidable if one wishes to get to other situations. But it is very difficult to acknowledge that oneself is to blame. So one looks for somebody else. Fortunately there are always people available. One can blame leaders, whether of the country or the firm or the church or anything. This scripture tells a timeless truth.

> *The land of Egypt . . . when we sat by
> the fleshpots and ate bread to the full*

Already the past has become bathed in rosy memory. The dark and ugly facts are forgotten. Egypt wasn't so bad after all. We have many versions of this. For some the country once enjoyed "good old days." For some the church once had a great "age of faith."

> *I will rain bread from heaven for you*

Even in the wilderness there are gifts received, nourishment found. It is different from the past, but it is there and its acceptance means life; its rejection can mean death.

Perhaps the really great lesson of this scripture is that God is as much with us in the wilderness as anywhere else, sometimes even more so. Consider the evidence about the quality of Christian community life in Eastern Europe, in societies in revolution, in famine belts.

> *Your murmurings are not against us but against the Lord*

Perhaps a modern application of this statement would be that very often the conscious focus of our anger, resentment, anxiety, or fear is not the real focus. The real focus and reason may be far deeper and should be probed and identified.

> *Come near before the Lord*

Very often in times of wilderness we fall away from worship with the community. That community, because it is changing in ways we find hard to understand, may be the very cause of our feeling in a wilderness! Yet this is the very reason to continue to ''come near before the Lord.''

> *They looked toward the wilderness, and the glory of the Lord appeared*

It was only when Israel looked toward the wilderness (faced it as a reality) that they could see God's glory (presence) in it.

Second Reading
Within this tortuous but closely reasoned piece of scripture, there is a real love for his own Jewish people expressed by Paul.

> *If their rejection means the reconciliation of the world*

There is no doubt that such language, later enshrined in Holy Scripture, was to have tragic consequences. Such consequences were, of course, totally unintended by Paul. However, the mere mention in the Bible of the word *rejection* gave legitimacy to all those down through history who wished to define the Jewish people as, at worst, outside humanity.

> *What will their acceptance mean but life from the dead?*

How obvious it is that this is what Paul longs for. How obvious also that, given the circumstances of the time, it was inconceivable that Judaism would take this new path. Today few would regard "rejection" and "acceptance" by God of his ancient people as hanging on their "rejection" or "acceptance" of Jesus of Nazareth as the Christ. Such a matter is coming to be based on a very different issue. We hear it expressed in Paul's own words.

> *The gifts and the call of God are irrevocable*

More and more Christian and Jewish relationships are being based on the recognition that the covenant made by God with his first people is an everlasting one. We do not have the right to regard that covenant as temporary or incomplete or needing its terms to be revised.

> *Just as you [Gentiles] were once diso-bedient . . . they have now been diso-bedient . . . God has consigned all men to disobedience that he may have mercy upon all*

Always Paul is anxious to see human events as having meaning and pattern within the purposes of God. Within that purpose both Gentile and Jew possess a role. It is becoming more and more a conviction in Christian thinking that this is the reality which must govern all future relationships between Christian and Jew.

Third Reading   *Jesus withdrew*

A straightforward acknowledgement of his humanity. Like any one of us he felt a need to withdraw, to carve out an island of time where pressure would be lifted.

> *A Canaanite woman . . . came out and cried, ''Have mercy''*

Because this journey was withdrawal from pressure and from the unceasing claim by others upon his time and energy, the approach of the woman is proof that withdrawal is not easy to achieve. We all know that so well. We know the frantic preparation to complete things before we leave for a holiday or even for a short break. We also know that another scramble is inevitable on our return, as we try to catch up with what has accumulated! All those feelings make the break itself something looked forward to and therefore jealously guarded!

> *He did not answer her a word*

We have all known this situation. The prospect of further involvement at this particular moment, as we begin a precious time of rest, appalls us. We don't reject the approach directly. We try to assess if we can possibly avoid it for the present. In modern terms we postpone returning the phone call, presuming that if it is not repeated it may lack urgency!

> *His disciples begged him, ''Send her away''*

When energy is low, nerves become frayed. The very repetition and shrillness of a human need can have the sad effect of turning any possible sympathy into actual revulsion.

> *I was sent only to the lost sheep of the house of Israel*

The weary human Galilean we see and hear at this moment is, like all of us sometimes, searching for a rationale for a decision he is uncomfortable with. In the depths of himself there are instincts demanding response to this woman. Other human elements in him cry out against response. He takes refuge for the moment in an exclusive Judaism. He defines the bounds of his own responsibility.

> *She came and knelt before him, saying, "Lord, help me"*

Every word communicates the poignancy of this moment. With shrewd intuition the woman moves from what may have been shrill crying, to the simple universal request which speaks from and to the heart of the human situation.

> *It is not fair to take the children's bread*

Already Jesus' instinct to respond is overcoming his first resolve that response might be avoided. He is still trying to shield himself behind a narrowly defined role, but is himself realizing the hollowness of this.

> *"Yes, Lord, yet even the dogs eat the crumbs*

It is a reply which pierces to the depths of Our Lord's being. She is saying that, even if she must crawl and grovel for recognition of her child's need, she will do so. Her love for her child, and her conviction that this man before her can help if he chooses, impell her to press him.

"O woman, great is your faith!"

The effect on a wary unresponsive Jesus is electric. Her reply releases in him all the wells of compassion, all the capacity for self-giving which will in time attain ultimate self-sacrifice. He becomes who he really is! Beyond weariness, beyond limitations and boundaries, the hidden Lord shines in and from the man. And the instrument of God to achieve this is a foreigner and a woman. She has become the channel of grace to him to whom millions look for grace.

Psalm

The nature of God is to give. In spite of the lack of human response, this is still true. The particular image which flashes out from this psalm for late twentieth-century Christians is the question, "Can God set a table in the wilderness?" In the midst of an age which has many of the properties of "wilderness," we possess the Christian altar or table as a resource for refreshment and nourishment while we serve God in a "wilderness" time.

Sunday between 21 and 27 August

Exodus 17:1–7
Romans 11:33–36
Matthew 16:13–20
Psalm: 95

Theme In all three readings we see human understanding trying to come to grips with something that defies full understanding. In the wilderness journey Israel and Moses find that there are few if any easy answers (Exodus). Paul suddenly feels over-whelmed by the unknowability of God (Romans), and the disciples trying desperately to express the baffling but irresistable reality they feel to be in their Master (Matthew).

First Reading   *All the congregation moved on from the wilderness by stages, according to the commandment of the Lord*

We eventually do move out of our wildernesses, whether we mean our own personal ex-periences or the life of a congregation or even of the whole church. It is very important to say this because we live at a time when many people feel that they are stranded in a vast wilderness and do not know which way to turn or whom to trust.

Perhaps the phrase ''by stages'' is very important. When we feel surrounded by wilderness, there is a feeling that there must be one single action or decision or plan, some-thing simple and instantaneous which can get us out into familiar territory again. To achieve this we are tempted to choose drastic and often simplistic solutions which eventually only compound the situation. On a personal level we may feel that the only solution for a seemingly impossible relationship is to get out of it, that the only solution for some doubt in our faith is to become fundamentalist or to give up the quest for faith entirely. On an organizational level a leader may feel that the only way out is to leave. A parish may feel the only way is to close down. None of these steps may be necessary in our experiences of wilderness if only we are prepared to realize that life is lived in stages and is essentially a journey in which there are very few short cuts, however desirable they may seem.

> *According to the commandment of the Lord*

Again a very significant phrase. It points out a very important and necessary attitude for any person or any group which feels itself to be in a wilderness time or situation. It is the realization that God is with us in the wilderness.

> *There was no water for the people to drink*

When we are experiencing wilderness, whether personally or in some organization we are part of, there is the feeling that there are no resources or, that if there are, we cannot find them. This feeling can make us accept defeat when we do not have to.

> *The people found fault with Moses*

It is human nature to look for a focus of blame in a wilderness situation. Most often it is directed at any available level of leadership.

Moses cried to the Lord

All leadership has its limitations. A leader must be allowed to express his or her frustration and fear and weariness. To do so is not weakness but possibly wisdom. The result can often be healing for all concerned.

Taking with you some of the elders of Israel

One of the most important steps any one in a leadership position can take is to begin to share it. Who knows, it may well have been the skill of one of these elders which lead to the discovery of water.

They put the Lord to the proof by saying, "Is the Lord among us or not?"

We cannot manipulate God — very often in life for very understandable reasons of fear or pain or sorrow, we try to. We make bargains with God, promising this if only we receive that. We make our trust conditional. We all do it. But such an attitude can never be the basis for a mature faith.

Second Reading   *O the depth of the riches and wisdom and knowledge of God*

Every so often, as he writes this or any other letter, something happens to Paul. Suddenly he will be overcome by a sense of the ultimacy of God. He will feel almost impertinent speaking of God, claiming to know this or that of God's thoughts or God's purposes. Such things, he will suddenly remind himself, are utterly beyond human minds to grasp. It is as if Paul, the scholar and theologian, springs up from where he sits writing, and adopts a position of pure helpless worship. It goes without saying that each one of us, whether we are preparing a homily or doing some Bible study, should be aware that those very same moments search for us. When they come, we should never regard them as merely distraction from the main task of getting answers to the meaning of a text. Such overwhelming moments are themselves the answer!

How unsearchable . . . how inscrutable

Many times in life there is a terrifying sense of those attributes of God. Particularly in the pain and suffering of life such words assume frightful dimensions. Why does this or that happen? Why must this or that be sacrificed so that something else may be achieved? Sometimes it is important to remind ourselves that faith is not measured by an ability to give answers. Sometimes faith can respond only by loving, patient presence.

*Who has known the mind of the Lord
. . . who has given a gift to him*

It is not accidental that in this particular moment Paul reaches back to two minds he has known all his life in the scriptures. First he echoes a question of Isaiah, then a question from the writer of the book of Job. Both speak out of a deeply mystical tradition. Both books express an attitude to God which in the end fully acknowledges human limitation in understanding.

To him be glory for ever

But such acknowledgement of human limitation does not end in a sense of defeat. It does not mean a defeated retreat from faith. The impenetrable glory of God is merely further ground for worship.

Third Reading   *Jesus came into the district of Caesarea Philippi*

Jesus is about to ask a key question of his disciples. It is interesting that he chooses to ask it while he and they are visiting one of the most worldly and (in our language) secularized cities he could have found. Caesarea Philippi was an army headquarters and also a large centre for the worship of the god Pan. In these two things we have images of two vast forces which pervade all contemporary experience, militarism and sexuality.

Who do men say that the Son of man is?

The question is asked by Jesus in that world of ancient pluralism, militarism, and sexuality. Doesn't that make it an extremely contemporary question? Such is the context of our lives. It is essential that we have some idea of the many attitudes to Jesus Christ which occupy the minds of today, both in and outside the church.

Some say John the Baptist, others say Elijah, others Jeremiah, others one of the prophets

On and on went the impressions and the scenarios, just as they do today. Jesus as teacher, as guru, as moral ethicist, as healer, as sentimentalized religious icon. Jesus as revolutionary, as freedom fighter, as political liberator. On and on the different images stream, each one to some extent a reflection of history and human experience in a certain place and time. All of them contain a truth.

Who do you say that I am?

Each of us in some sense at some moment must receive that question if our Christian faith is to become real and mature. I must at some point decide who Jesus of Nazareth is for me. I must say it. That means the decision must be conscious and intentional.

You are the Christ

Like Peter we do not have to understand in a precise and analytical way what we are saying. Indeed, we never fully will understand. The depths of Jesus Christ will for ever elude us.

On this rock I will build my church

But on such conscious and intentional attitudes is a solid personal faith built. This personal faith, with others like it, will form a resilient Christian community.

Psalm

Again we are expressing the glory of God, an essentially undefinable glory beyond our understanding. Understood or not it is the overriding reality as a people wrestles with a wilderness journey. Whatever happens they affirm that God is their God and that they are God's people (v 7). There will always be unanswerable questions. Why are some waters bitter and others sweet? We even use that very language to describe life. We say it can be bitter-sweet. Yet in the face of the inscrutabilities of life, there is a determination not to harden the heart in response but to keep it open to faith.

Sunday between 28 August and 3 September

Exodus 19:1–9
Romans 12:1–13
Matthew 16:21–28
Psalm 114

Theme At the heart of human experience and history is the choice to live and act in a relationship with God. A people makes that choice as Israel finds itself deep in the wilderness of Sinai (Exodus). We hear Paul asking us to realize that we are called to give ourselves into a living body with others who are likewise committing themselves to be Christ's body (Romans). Our Lord describes the same fundamental choice we must make, to give integrity to the central core of our being by following him (Matthew).

First Reading

The people of Israel had gone forth out of the land of Egypt

If we are ready to see the journey of the people of Israel as a pattern of our human journey, then we can see many truths about ourselves in the events of that long-ago journey. The first truth is, that in so far as Egypt was home to them, even with its grim conditions,

they had to leave it. It doesn't matter at the moment why.
What is significant is that their having to leave the familiar
is an unavoidable part of our own experience.

I brought you to myself

So God wishes his people to realize that
the events they have been through, the journey thus far,
is in response to God's call. But whether we realize it or
not, this is true of our own lives. Life lived in the context
of faith in God is lived as response to God's call. Wherever
and whatever I may be, I am at this moment being called
onward to some deepening, to some growing, to something
more. The final depth of the calling is that I am being called by God to a relationship with God.

I bore you on eagles' wings

There is an extraordinary mingling of
power and gentleness in this image. There are moments in
life when one experiences being borne up. It is not present
always, nor should we seek it always. Soaring spiritually
is possible only because much of our journey must be done
at an earthbound level. A wish to soar always, a feeling of
guilt if one is not perpetually ''high,'' can be exhausting
and self-defeating.

All that the Lord has spoken we will do

To live in the trust that the sequence of
one's life, its decisions and directions, are all a response
to a deep call of God, is to inculcate in us a wish to be obedient. It is to see our wills as acting with another and greater
will. Such an attitude is a deeply integrating factor in one's
life.

I am coming to you in a thick cloud

Possessing a sense of guidance from God is not easy. There are times, even with the best trust we can have, that we feel God is hidden in a thick cloud. Conflicting voices, loyalties, wishes, and arguments can very much cloud the issue (we even use that image in everyday conversation). But above all, there is the fact that God *is* in that cloud. A purpose exists for us. We are not floundering alone.

Second Reading   *I appeal to you . . . to present your bodies as sacrifice, . . . spiritual worship*

The totality of our lives is given to us only to give back to God. That does not mean that there is a section of our lives called the "spiritual." All the tangible things of life — job, possessions, bodies, sexuality, appetites — are potential for our giving to God.

Do not be conformed to this world, but transformed

More than ever today it is a struggle not to be devoured by a culture and forced to conform and respond to its stimuli, its temptations, and its standards. To resist needs not only good intentions and feelings but also thought and our critical faculties ("your mind").

Everyone . . . to think . . . according to the measure of faith which God has assigned him [or her]

As he would do many times, Paul appeals to an early congregation not to be weakened by the alienations which spring from self-centred and ego-conscious individualism.

> *We, though many, are one body in Christ*

We receive a picture of Christian society which has endured as an immensely inspired image and has become refocused for us in this century. When we struggle to gather as followers of Our Lord, aware of the differences which exist even within a single congregation, it is more necessary than ever that we respond to this image of being "one body in Christ."

> *Individually members of one another*

In a society of much loneliness and much emotional need, not to mention economic need, it is increasingly necessary to hear Paul pointing to our mutual need of one another's care. This realization in parish life is creating more and more pastoral lay ministry.

> *Having gifts that differ . . . let us use them*

Again there is a glorious recapturing of this concept in Christian congregational life today. Instead of looking to an official source of all gifts (which of course does not exist!), we see gifts of the most diverse kind scattered among us, and not one is to be dismissed by another.

> *With zeal . . . outdo one another*

The continual plea of Paul for the use of any human gift is that it be given fully and generously and joyfully!

Third Reading   *Must suffer many things . . . be killed . . . be raised*

This kind of statement would later in the church's life become the basis and sequence for its creeds. They contain threat and shock for those who hear them. These facts at the heart of the faith always come as unwelcome, whether in Bible study or liturgy. In some sense we all react as Peter did.

> *God forbid Lord! This shall never happen to you*

Peter's very natural response is one of denial. All of us in various ways can practise the same element of denial about both life and Christian faith. There can be a neurotic ability to deny the dark possibilities in and for ourselves. We will never be sick or be bereaved or grow old! Others all around us but not us! Acceptance of such things is one of the challenges to our maturity. In fact all such elements of life can serve as vehicles coming to terms with our own mortality. We can deny the reality of such shadows in the Gospel by insisting on hearing only its pleasant and attractive elements. Our Lord's words to Peter are salutary.

> *You are a hindrance to me! You are not on the side of God*

An inability in us to face and name realities is a deadly hindrance to our own development and performance. Such an unreality in our attitude is not compatible with what God wishes us to become. It is not an element of the Holy Spirit in us but an element of our fearful self-centred humanity which so desperately needs that Holy Spirit.

> *If any man would come after me*

In response to Peter, Our Lord defines the way of realism. There is a cross to be taken up. To say this is not to paint life in depressing colours but to state the reality of life.

Let him deny self

What is involved is the acknowledgement that the self is not the centre of the universe, nor does the universe of other lives revolve around the centre of our particular needs and wishes. Taking the cross has to do with giving oneself rather than taking, accepting responsibility rather than refusing it.

And follow me

It means, too, centring on a self beyond one's own self. It means the focus becoming that of Jesus as Lord, whose own carrying of a cross produces a life so vibrant and real that neither time nor familiarity dims it!

Whoever would save his life will lose it

The great paradox at the heart of all human choices about life. Hoarded, guarded, self-oriented life shrivels. It goes on, but it does so diminished and self-defeated. Risked, expended, offered beyond itself, life can be demanding and costly, yet it can also flower and grow and be infinitely rewarding. Jesus says to us that, if life is offered to be lived on his terms, we can find ultimate reward. We see such ultimate self-offering in great souls who shine in the world of their time.

What shall a man give in return for his life?

We are not talking about mere physical existence, nor about something detached from it called spiritual life. Our Lord is asking a question about the most profound choice we have to make. In some lives it can be a decision made at a particular moment, in others it emerges as the sum total of many seemingly minor choices. It is the decision concerning to whom or to what we give the essential core of our being. The reason why this is so all important is that we are accountable for our decision when "the Son of man is to come with his angels in the glory of his Father."

Psalm

When Israel as a people came out of Egypt, there evolved a relationship with God. Something of the same can be said for each of us as we emerge into adulthood. A relationship exists with God. We have to choose whether we wish to recognize it, and then whether we wish to foster it. We would do well to recognize its incalculable value as an element in our lives. Using the language of scripture, we would do well to "tremble at the presence of the Lord."

Sunday between 4 and 10 September

Exodus 19:16–24
Romans 13:1–10
Matthew 18:15–20
Psalm 115:1–11

Theme All the scriptures today are about some element of ''encounter.'' Moses is summoned to an encounter with God (Exodus). Paul speaks to the community in Rome about their constant and unavoidable encountering the civil powers of the society (Romans). Jesus speaks of the way we are able to handle difficult and painful personal encounters (Matthew).

First Reading

As we move through these Exodus readings we are seeing the journey of Israel as a pattern of our personal human journey. This is by no means the only way to see this wilderness saga, but in the homilies of this year we have made this choice.

> *Thunders and lightenings, a thick cloud, a very loud trumpet blast . . . all the people trembled*

The nature of human experience is that we must come to crises. We know that they lie waiting for us. Most often we try very hard to avoid them, but as we move through the unpredictabilities and the complexities of life, they spring on us without warning. Only in retrospect do we realize that the ingredients of the crisis had been gathering over a long period of time.

> *Moses brought the people out of the camp to meet God*

There is a sense in which all crisis points of life are a meeting with God. They are certainly a meeting with our deepest selves, and in that sense we discover what depth of God's grace, or what depth of relationship with God, is ours. As we watch Israel move ''out of the camp,'' we realize that sometimes to deal with crises we need to move aside from the normal business of our lives, to get some quietness or even solitariness, to look for what inner resources we have and what responses we should make. As they moved ''out of the camp'' and ''took their stand,'' so we need a place and a time to take our stand.

> *The whole mountain quaked*

We even speak of our problems being ''mountainous'' as they dwarf our capacity to deal with them.

> *The Lord came down on Mount Sinai*

Yet the whole point of this great crisis moment is that the presence of God is here. This is not a crisis of destruction but of new creation. It is, though they do not yet know it, an encounter which will broaden and enrich their whole future (and ours). Which is precisely the truth which can be present in the crisis moments of our experience.

*The Lord called Moses to the top of the
mountain, and Moses went up. The Lord
said to Moses, ''Go down and warn the
people''*

Sometimes we are called to experience
heights of the spirit (mountain-top moments). And there
is with us too a need for warning. Intense spiritual experience can be transforming, exhilarating, exhausting, a
source of joy, a source of anxiety. That may sound strange,
but the presence of God is something our humanity is not
wholly designed for. That's the tragedy being expressed
when we speak of our humanity as flawed or sinful.

*Go down, and come up bringing Aaron
with you*

For our encounters with God, we too
need a companion to come up the mountain with us. If it
can be someone who has himself or herself been on the
mountains of God, then all the better. Today we call such
a person a ''spiritual director,'' but such a gift can sometimes
be found in a friend. There are ''Aarons'' in disguise around
us in unexpected places!

Second Reading

Perhaps no other passage in the New
Testament has caused so much heart searching for twentieth-century Christians involved in the turmoil and struggle of many societies in our time.

*Let every person be subject to the gov-
erning authorities. He who resists the
authorities resists what God has
appointed*

I have made the above extract, but the theme is sounded in the whole first half of the reading. Perhaps the best way to respond is to point to some magnificient Christian social responsibility carried out in this century. We recall the agony Dietrich Bonhoeffer went through in deciding that he would ally himself with those who plotted against Hitler's life. We cosider Lanani Louwum, the martyred archbishop of Uganda, who felt impelled by Christian conviction to confront his president Idi Amin. The list is long in our century. It includes Martin Luther King Jr and all who have chosen non-violent protest against what they perceived to be unjust social legislation. It includes the thousands who protest decisions about nuclear arms, and those in totalitarian regimes where it is difficult to see how resisting those in authority is rejecting "what God has appointed."

> *One must be subject . . . for the sake of conscience*

But there seem to be circumstances (to be discovered by early Christians very soon after Paul's writing this) where precisely for the sake of Christian conscience one cannot be subject.

> *Respect to whom respect is due, honour to whom honour is due*

Here Paul's statements make choice more possible. There are now criteria for evaluation of the authority. In Christian terms, are respect and honour due?

> *He who loves his neighbour has fulfilled the law*

Here again there is greater freedom for choice of response in a political regime. The highest law of all is love for neighbour. Having to ask "who is my neighbour?" in agonized circumstances of political crisis, the Christian must choose a course of action for that neighbour's good as it can be discerned at the time.

Love does no wrong to a neighbour

If in the agony of South African society white Christian conscience decides to identify black acquaintances as "neighbour," how is "love to do no wrong"? What is the "right" for love to do. Any such searching for the right action of love of neighbour must at some stage refuse to be "subject to the governing authorities." Paul plainly says that to act so as to avoid "wrong to a neighbour" is "the fulfilling of the law." Such a law supersedes all other law for a Christian.

Third Reading   *If your brother sins against you, go and tell him his fault*

Behind the deceptively simple admonition is a great challenge and great wisdom. The challenge lies in the fact that personal confrontation is something few enjoy, and many will do a great deal to avoid. When we do manage to pluck up the courage to do it, we need skill and sensitivity if the meeting is to serve a positive purpose. In recent years much work has been done to help people to handle such an encounter so that their protest against a felt wrong or hurt is heard by the "brother" or "sister" (who of course may also be friend or colleague). It is also important that the conversation makes possible a continued and even improved relationship afterwards. As Jesus says,

If he listens to you, you have gained a brother

And, in that case, the relationship has a future, even possibly an enhanced one.

But if he does not listen

Every possible effort is to be made to avoid a final breach. The next stage of encounter may be greatly helped by the presence of a very small and trusted group. Both sides can be heard and what is heard can be checked by others less involved. Both parties may learn they have unrealized agenda.

Tell it to the church

In contemporary society that statement could mean a larger group of friends within a congregation. This is possible if a network of trust and affection has been built up. After all, such involvement of carefully chosen friends is an extension of their regular exchanging of the Peace. It could be a test of the reality of that. Only if this fails, does Our Lord accept the breakdown of relationship.

Where two or three are gathered in my name, there am I in the midst of them

The words ''in my name'' are important. If two people who share the fellowship of the faith must work through a situation of strained and troubled relationship, there is no reason why such an encounter cannot be offered in prayer and the presence of Our Lord recalled. To do this the presence of a third party might well be desirable, to avoid any feeling that the person suggesting the prayer is trying to manipulate the situation or trying in some way to occupy higher moral ground! This scripture may seem to emerge out of forms of Christian community no longer available to us in today's society. I suggest this need not be true where bonds of real community have been forged in a parish.

Psalm

Again and again voices in the scriptures contrast the ultimacy of God with the futility of idols. The contemporary equivalent for us is to hold up the ultimacy of God as the focus of our energies, our faith, and our allegiance, and to contrast such a faith with the futility of lesser allegiances — power, possessions.

Sunday between 11 and 17 September

Exodus 20:1–20
Romans 14:5–12
Matthew 18:21–35
Psalms 19:7–14

Theme A common theme in all three scriptures is that of bondage or imprisonment. The key to Israel continuing to live in freedom after the bondage of Egypt is their continued obedience toward the law of God (Exodus). The key to avoid the prison of isolation and alienation in community life is to give honour to the views and positions of others (Romans). The key to avoid becoming the prisoner of one's own hatreds and resentments is to be a forgiving person (Matthew).

First Reading

We are present at the moment of infinite significance. The substance of these verses speaks at every level of human experience, personal and social. It is true for the individual, the community, the nation, the whole of humanity.

No other gods before me

The only reality we are to accord ultimate value is God. This is easily said, but we are constantly drawn to do otherwise.

You shall not make yourself a graven image

Why? Because we are often inclined to do so. We make some other lesser element of life an ultimate value for ourselves; then we pursue it with all our energy — "bow down to it and serve it."

You shall not take the name of the Lord your God in vain

We have many and subtle and very often unconscious ways of using God for our own ends. Sometimes "electronic religion," as we call it, is tempted to false uses of God's promises and God's grace under the pressures of keeping up a television empire. On a personal level we would be taking God's name in vain if, for instance, we falsely professed faith in God to further a personal or business relationship for our own gain. All discrepancies between what we profess and what we perform are a taking of God's name in vain.

Remember the sabbath day, to keep it holy

I like the language of Harper's Bible Dictionary at this point (page 1033 in the new edition). "The commandment to set one day apart from all others stands as a bulwark against endless self-destructive human greed and spares Israel the horror of being a Sabbathless culture." That issue is before almost every community of any size in our culture.

Honour your father and your mother

A statement about the relationship between the past, present, and future. It says many things.

Among them it tells us that the present is not an isolated moment. We would be wise to know how we got here in order to shape how we try to go on from here. If we seek hope, then we had better begin by seeking memory. In a word, this commandment speaks of tradition.

> *You shall not kill*

Our century has come to realize that this must go far beyond individual violence. This speaks to the terrible arsenals which lie hidden in the earth, sail beneath the seas, and float above us in space. In these our own inventions we have captured the means of ultimate violence.

> *You shall not commit adultery . . . you shall not steal . . . you shall not bear false witness . . . you shall not covet*

All of which are, in different guises, a doing of violence to professed loyalties, to legitimate ownership, to the integrity of justice in a society. The last commandment has a peculiar significance for our age with its vast organizations dedicated solely to ensuring that all of us covet, from the cradle to the grave, as we carry out our role of "consumer"!

Second Reading

Anyone who thinks of Paul as narrow and dogmatic should take note of this passage. We listen to a gracious and liberal voice begging for the same graciousness and liberality among the Christian communities coming to birth.

> *One man esteems one day as better than another, while another esteems all days alike*

It could be an appeal by the mayor of a huge modern city that the "holy day" of each segment of the population be given mutual respect. The secularized majority regard "all days alike."

> *He who eats . . . he who abstains . . .*
> [*both*] *in honour of the Lord*

Religious practices do not bestow a moral superiority. Motivation is what counts. If a lifestyle is consciously offered to God in an attitude of stewardship of one's life, then God is served.

> *If we live . . . if we die . . .* [*it is*] *to the Lord*

All our differences of attitude, lifestyle, and practice within the Christian community are minor compared with the fact that we are one within the creation of God and within our relationships (which may vary greatly) to Jesus Christ.

> *Why . . . pass judgement on your brother? We shall all stand before the judgement seat of God*

Our constant human temptation is to pass judgement, especially where there are differences of any kind. At present there is a great deal of such mutual judgement being done in the vast spectrum of contemporary Christianity, between and within fundamentalist, evangelical, and mainline churches. Yet all our traditions and liturgies and activities fall equally short of the glory of God.

Third Reading   *Lord, how often? As many as seven times*

This is Peter at his eager-to-please best. In suggesting that one should forgive seven times, he was going far beyond even the highest demands of his time and culture. Because of that we can imagine the way in which Our Lord's reply pulls everyone up short. Jesus is actually suggesting that forgiveness be without limit! We see Jesus being totally consistent with his treatment of other such issues. Again and again life is presented to Jesus as a thing of contracts, precisely measured and codified, setting limits to behaviour. Again and again he changes the whole way of looking at human life. He goes deep inside the human situation. Someone asks him a question about the legalities of violence, and Jesus moves from violent action to the interior source of violence we call hatred.

Not seven times but seventy times seven

Jesus switches from limitations to ultimacy by using Peter's categories but shattering them. Jesus asks that we cease to calculate forgiveness and begin to be forgiving. To drive it home he turns to a story.

The kingdom of heaven

When Jesus speaks of the kingdom, he is seeking images for the way reality is, deep down in the heart of things where God rules. In the story which Our Lord now tells, the king is God, of course, and the servants are each one of us.

One . . . who owed him 10,000 talents

The debt is a colossal sum. Did Jesus use it deliberately to get across what my humanity "owes" to

God? The image immediately communicates the impossibility of my doing any moral posturing, any claiming to possess superior moral position. Before God I am naked. Yet I am offered a relationship. If I really am aware what the Christian faith is saying to me, then I begin to realize the pathetic nature of my rights and the incalculable generosity I have received in spite of that. I am loved, given grace, led to a loving community and to loving relationships which give meaning and integration to my life. I am given what the ageless prayer calls "the means of grace and the hope of glory." I am forgiven my spiritual penury.

That same servant went out

I am that servant. I continually refuse to forgive fully even though I myself have received forgiveness. Here Our Lord communicates an insight that psychology points to in our own age. The mere fact that the servant condemns another so soon after his own debt has been forgiven shows that he has actually not registered the fact of that forgiveness. Put another way, we cannot ourselves feel forgiven unless we forgive. The inability to forgive, the resentment and even hatred which that inability creates, actually rebounds on ourselves. It imprisons us, as the king in the parable orders the unforgiving man to be imprisoned. The peculiar irony of our prison is that it is self-erected and self-secured, while we ourselves hold the key of freedom within the cell of our tightly held resentment.

Psalm

This hymn of praise to the law of God presents that law not as something superimposed on our humanity but as something which fosters and enriches all human activity and intercourse. Obedience to the law does not limit life but enhances it. It even penetrates beneath our conscious mind to the subconscious ("my secret faults"). Above all, it reminds one continually that one's own humanity is not the ultimate reference point (it keeps one from presumptuous sins).

Sunday between 18 and 24 September

Exodus 32:1–14
Philippians 1:21–27
Matthew 20:1–16
Psalm 106:7–8,
19–23

Theme There is a common thread through the scriptures in terms of the generosity of God. In the wilderness Israel deserves punishment for their reversion to the primitive, yet they receive the trust of a remade covenant (Exodus). Paul discovers that in spite of imprisonment he is given a joy and a sense of achievement so rich as to be almost inexpressible (Philippians). Jesus points to God as one whose justice goes beyond contract and calculation (Matthew).

First Reading *Up, make us gods, who shall go before us*

Societies have a hunger for gods to go before them. In a wilderness time there is a desperate hunger for gods. It's interesting to name some of them. The god of economic prosperity? The god of national security? In a time of uncertainty we seek the god of certain and simple answers. There are some very dark gods such as the god of race.

> *This Moses, the man who brought us up out of Egypt*

What Moses represents is the more difficult challenge in life. He represents journey and risk, uncertainty, the necessity for trust, the tough call to community. Given half a chance (such as his prolonged absence in this situation) the people jettison this challenging agenda.

> *Aaron received the gold . . . and made a golden calf*

Whatever symbolic meaning we give to the golden calf (for them it was a memory of a familiar Egyptian cult), it was a diminishing of themselves, an instinctive reversion to a former lower existence. If we experience a temptation to take refuge in materialism, to become passive consumers in a "consumer society," then that too is a self-diminishment for us.

> *These are your gods, O Israel, who brought you up out of the land of Egypt*

This is of course a massive lie. It is what Orwell called "double think." The worship of possessions, the celebration of appetite are the very things which do not bring a culture or a community from slavery to freedom. Mere appetite (consumerism) ensures that they remain in "slavery."

> *The Lord said to Moses . . . "let me alone . . . that I may consume them."*
> *But Moses besought the Lord*

The rest of this reading is an intense dialogue between God and Moses. In it we see the great Jewish insight we call Covenant. The betrayal that human nature is capable of, our refusal to be faithful to responsibility, breaks the trust between us and God. Our secular way of regarding history makes it difficult for us to see things this way, yet if we claim to be a biblical people we cannot ignore it.

I [God] have promised

In spite of our human betrayals God remains true to the covenant. In our present wilderness of history, as we stand before another mushroom cloud, like and yet unlike that hanging over Sinai, it is absolutely essential that we be aware of the biblical covenant because it can energize and inspire us in the terror of these times.

Second Reading

We are entering Paul's mind at a very intense time. He is in prison, never knowing when, in a most literal sense, the axe is going to fall.

To me to live is Christ and to die is gain

In a deep and lovely sense Paul no longer exists. He has handed over his "self" to Our Lord so readily and fully that he has "put on Christ" (to use a phrase Paul uses elsewhere). It is becoming immaterial to him whether or not he is to live. In fact, there is at times "a desire to depart."

To remain in the flesh is more necessary

Paul is not expressing some suicidal depression. He has become that rare being, a person who feels free to accept death or to continue full living. The driving force for future life is the Christian communities he has begun, especially the community of Philippi.

> *In me you may have ample cause to
> glory in Christ Jesus*

Paul's wish to live is to give the community cause to glorify God. For Paul the church is everything, even reason for life itself. So often we feel that someone can identify overmuch with some cause or institution. Yet, if our commitment is a healthy one, it can be extremely energizing, giving our lives focus and meaning, taking our lives far beyond the self and its demands.

> *Firm in one spirit, with one mind striving side by side*

The necessity for unity is never far from Paul's mind. He had ample cause to be saddened by the fragility of Christian community, its tendency to be fractious and bitter in its divisions. It is a problem particularly near us today as we try to contain a rampant individualism of many visions and hopes all set in a context of anxiety.

Third Reading

A story with many levels of meaning about God's dealing with our humanity and our varied responses.

> *Early in the morning . . . about the
> third hour . . . about the sixth and
> ninth hour . . . about the eleventh hour*

God is one who continually calls into his service. If the daylight hours are seen as an image of a human life-cycle, then we see a God whose call is lifelong, responded to by some in the "morning" of life, by some at the height of their powers, by some at "the eleventh hour." This image in turn links in with our increased recognition that spirituality is itself a lifelong process. In turn, that recognition has brought into parish life a realization that Christian education should reach out to all ages in the community.

> *Pay them their wages beginning with the last up to the first*

There is a familiar sound here. It is the echo of something heard many times in Our Lord's ministry. However expressed in different images on different occasions, it always hints at an essential contradiction of the ways of the world by the ways of the kindgom of God. Poverty in the world becomes riches in the kingdom. First in the world becomes last in the kingdom. It is as if we are being told that, whatever the kingdom is, it challenges and sometimes totally contradicts the values and methods of the present age.

> *Those hired about the eleventh hour . . . each received a denarius. When the first came . . . each of them received also a denarius*

We need to know a point of fact to see a deep meaning for contemporary Christianity in this moment. A denarius was a basic day's wage. It was minimal for the support of a worker and family. Anything less was almost useless. In the story the householder contracts only with the first people hired. With each succeeding shift there is no contract. There could have been a very oppressive contract, given the increasing possibility of a day of unemployment as the day wore on. With each passing hour the employer held more and more cards in his hand. Yet these cards, this power to victimize, is not used. Again a category of the kingdom is shown as totally different from that of society, either then or now.

> *I choose to give to this last as I give to*
> *you [the first]*

The householder gives to the last workers what he knows is minimal for human need for a day. Anything less is useless. With the first workers there is an actual contract. He lives up to that. With the later and last workers there is an agreement based on trust. It has all the fragility of such agreements. In today's economy we see many such agreements (based on trust) brutally betrayed. But in the story the householder abides by the trust. The message of Jesus surely is that God is essentially a God of justice.

Psalm

These verses echo the theme that is clear in the Exodus and Matthew passages. The love of God is not tied to our desserts. We may "defy" God (as "at the Red Sea"). We may "forget God (v 21). Yet the response of God is to offer again a continuing covenant relationship.

Sunday between 25 September and 1 October

Exodus 33:12–23
Philippians 2:1–13
Matthew 21:28–32
Psalm 99

Theme A common theme is the quality of our servanthood to God. We see and hear Moses, exhausted and dispirited, yet still prepared to stay with the task (Exodus). We hear Paul asserting once again that the greatness of Our Lord is in his ability to be a servant (Philippians). We then hear Our Lord himself pointing out that performing a service, albeit grudgingly, is better than accepting a task and reneging on it (Matthew).

First Reading

Throughout this passage we are aware that a great crisis moment has just passed. The law has been given. The dark side of Israel has emerged in the making of the golden calf. Its consequences are still uncalculated. We are looking at Moses as one exhausted. Reaction has set in, as it does with us all after our resources have been utterly taxed.

Thou sayest, "Bring up this people,"
but thou hast not let me know whom
thou wilt send with me

We can hear the petulance of a tired, dispirited man who carries great responsibility. He is saying that he has been given a job but not been given the support to do it.

> *You [God] have said, "You [Moses] have found favour in my sight"*

Moses feels that there have been praise and affirmation, yet somehow support is lacking in real terms. This can very often be true in our experience, particularly in our professional lives. We can be affirmed in a job while at the same time be used and manipulated by our not being given support and resources to do it.

> *Consider too that this nation is thy people*

We can hear resentment now. Moses is not impressed by God's performance lately! One of the very refreshing elements in Jewish spirituality is the freedom to grumble to God about his performance! Even anger at God is allowed. Christians tend to draw back from such expression, yet we still feel such an anger deep down.

> *My presence will go with you, and I will give you rest*

Notice the acknowledgement by God that Moses needs rest. Our humanity is known to its creator. We do not have to pretend powers and abilities we do not have. We do not have to hide that we become tired and dispirited.

> *If thy presence will not go with me, do not carry us up from here*

That statement is the measure of Moses' depression. It is a cry we all know. "I can't carry on!" We can be overcome by a feeling that we are alone, without support.

I know you by name

The response sounding within Moses is the quiet but absolute promise of God, guaranteeing his presence in the journey ahead. It is the response we are given as we in our own experience have this dialogue with a God who seems absent.

Moses said, "Show me thy glory"

It is a very human but dangerous request. It is human because Moses wants some sign to shore himself up in his present weary doubts. It is dangerous because it smacks of something we hear forbidden elsewhere in scripture — testing God. But this time a favour is granted.

I will be gracious to whom I will be gracious

There is a mystery here we all know as we observe human life. Sometimes people are given a sign, an encouraging message, when faith has just been newborn or when it is still fragile after a period of doubt and/or exhaustion.

Man shall not see me and live

Such signs are always mediated in the ordinary. A friend will make a remark, a letter will be received, there will be a dream. God communicates through the ordinary because only in that way can our humanity receive him.

You shall see my back

All human concepts of God are partial. How changed the sometimes terrible history of religion would be if this had always been remembered. Moses is a symbol of even the greatest and wisest humanity as he crouches in a rock-face to protect himself from the ultimate glory of God. He is rewarded by a fleeting glimpse of that glory, knowing that that is all his humanity is capable of experiencing.

Second Reading *Being of the same mind, having the same love, being in full accord and of one mind*

The frequency with which Paul pleads for the quality of community life is an indication that Christian community was no easier to achieve in those early days than it is now! Of course, the very intensity with which the new faith was being discovered made for an intense communal life in the church. The reason that is significant for us is that we too experience intense Christian communal life precisely for the same reason. We are living in a time of rediscovered faith in many lives.

In humility count others better than yourselves

An echo of the problem in Corinth. The early communities drew into them those of every class who were hungry for meaning and hope. It was only natural that there would be some elements of snobbery. It's interesting that Paul doesn't merely say, "Count yourselves less than others." That tactic is artificial anyway. But, like Our Lord,

Paul asks for a deep change of consciousness. Without diminishing in any way our own self image, even continuing to rejoice and affirm our own gifts and abilities, we accord the gifts and abilities of others an even greater worth! Humility is not denying one's own self-worth, it is according greater worth to another.

> *Have this mind among yourselves which is yours in Christ Jesus*

There is a simple yet very profound question that we Christians might ask more frequently than we do. "What would the mind of Our Lord be about this situation"? It is an important question because we claim to be the body of Christ. This image is frequently used. We tend to be so familiar with it that its meaning becomes diminished. If we are indeed his body, then his mind must be found in that body. His attitudes, his way of dealing with people, his consciousness of God, his sense of justice — all must be discerned somewhere in the corporate "mind" of his "body" the church.

> *Emptied himself, taking the form of a servant*

Again, not for the first time in the scripture record, Our Lord's greatness is seen in terms of servanthood.

> *Obedient unto death*

His servanthood actually extends to the ultimate level of becoming "servant" to death. There is a reason why this text is important today in our culture. We wish in many ways to be masters of death — to postpone it, to defy it, to disguise it. This struggle is not wrong, but at some stage we have to make decisions about our "obedience to death," above all when and at what stages we offer that obedience.

Third Reading   *Two sons*

For Our Lord, an image of two kinds of human beings, also two kinds of religion. The original setting is that of a society where there is a great deal of official piety. Its practice of formal religion hides a great deal of cynicism. On the other hand, many in society have no religious pretensions ("tax collectors and harlots") but are hungry for some spiritual foundations in their lives and are prepared to respond if it is offered in terms they can relate to.

The same is true today. Frequently in the community of a church you will have those for whom the church — its affairs, its organization, its internal politics, its petty power struggles — have become everything. They are a substitute for faith. In the same community one will have people who, perhaps for the first time, have glimpsed the person of Our Lord and the thrilling tantalizing outlines of a kingdom which beckons them. They may need much help. They will need relationships they can respond to, a language they can hear.

There are, of course, other levels on which this story operates. A very straightforward dimension of it points out quite simply that to produce even grudgingly is far better than cheerfully promising and then producing nothing! This latter image might well serve to set us thinking about a very necessary aspect of today's church — the question of responsible and accountable (as distinct from casual and irresponsible) volunteerism.

Psalm

A portrait of God as very much the ruler of life, the source of authority, before whom our role is that of servants ("confess his name," "fall down before his footstool''). Even the greatest of human lives are merely ser-vants (Moses, Aaron, Samuel). In fact, their recognition of themselves as servants is the source of the stature!

Sunday between 2 and 8 October

Numbers 27:12–23
Philippians 3:12–21
Matthew 21:33–43
Psalm 81:1–10

Theme A common theme is that of God's calling people to service and ministry. In the journey of Israel a successor to Moses must be found, and Joshua is called (Numbers). Paul makes clear that God calls from beyond us, from our future. We are called to journey farther and to become more (Philippians). In his biting parable Our Lord warns that God can sometimes call and use people to whose gifts we are blind (Matthew).

First Reading *Go up into this mountain of Abarim and see the land*

What comes as a literal command to Moses long ago is also a command to us as Christians. If we wish to see the Christian faith and hope as a whole, or to become aware of it in greater depth and with greater clarity, we have to spend some moments on a mountain top. Now, while we cannot have "mountain top" experiences just when we want them, it is possible to place ourselves in situations of quietness or prayer or retreat, where we can receive them if they come. The problem in most lives is that we don't take time to do any spiritual mountain climbing.

When you have seen it, you also shall be gathered to your people

While for Moses this statement is a message about the ending of his life, for us there can be another nuance of meaning. If we do have moments of deep and rich experience of Christian faith, perhaps a sense of the presence of Christ or a flash of insight about a piece of scripture, the effect of it is to make richer our membership in a Christian community. In that sense it gathers us to our people.

You shall be gathered to your people . . . because you rebelled against my word

The episode in question occurred earlier in Moses' life. I don't think it lessens this scripture to say that we do not think of God today in this way. There may have been a deep feeling of guilt in Moses himself. In us all there is regret and guilt, the longing to have done some things differently. But the unchanging power in this scripture is the reminder that all our decisions and actions add up finally to form us and to define the totality of our lives. Every decision made, every seeming success or seeming failure, every choice small and large has brought us for good or for ill to where we are.

Moses said, ''Let the Lord appoint a man''

Moses shows greatness as he unhesitatingly sets outs to ensure continuity. So often it is human nature to hang on to authority or leadership a little longer. Deep down we think our vision and our contribution of ultimate importance. But far greater is the design of God, of which our role is a small part.

> *Take Joshua . . . invest him with some of your authority*

The important word is "some." We cannot control the future according to our way or our view of our methods. Moses can only pass on "some" of his authority because there must be room for Joshua's own different authority.

> *He laid his hands upon him and commissioned him*

Suddenly we can identify with this moment, if hands have been laid on us by someone in the Christian community. Joshua is commissioned for ministry in the wilderness. So are we.

Second Reading   *Not that I am already perfect, but I press on*

This complete first sentence of the reading is a beautiful and moving description of a Christian's relationship with Jesus Christ. We have not (nor will we ever in this life) reached the heights which Our Lord scaled, but we keep climbing. The reason we keep climbing (to continue the mountaineering image) is that we are roped to our Lord by ties such as baptism.

> *Forgetting what lies behind, and straining forward*

One couldn't find a better expression of a healthy attitude to life. Behind us all is a great mixture of lived experience, joyful and painful, positive and negative. One is not to deny this but to accept it, to be aware that we are accepted by God in spite of it all and that it is the journey from here on which counts. God is not digging around the lower levels of our climb, assessing old mistakes and lamenting half-forgotten detours and falls. God is a voice whose call, Paul realizes, is an "upward call," a call from higher up which encourages and energizes us to respond. To see life in such terms of anticipation rather than remembrance, possibility rather than regret, is to be "mature," Paul says.

> *Many . . . whose god is the belly . . .*
> *they glory in their shame, with minds*
> *set on earthly things*

The immature lifestyle is obsessed with appetite and its constant restlessness. Christian faith does not condemn the worldly. It condemns a sad materialistic obsession which is blind to other levels of reality beyond the material and beyond the self. A healthy Christian life rejoices in things, including one's own body and the many indescribably beautiful aspects of creation and human experience. At the same time, these can never be made ultimate because the ultimate is "not yet."

Third Reading   *There was a householder who planted a vineyard*

Anyone hearing Our Lord tell this parable knew that it was a very precise attack on the religious establishment of his day and of his own people. So it is quite proper for us to apply the parable to our own Christian community life or to the church as a whole. In what sense are we being responsible tenants (stewards) in the vineyard (the church) of God?

> *He sent his servants*

How do we use human beings in the church? There are a host of possible questions here, depending on what categories of ''servants'' we wish to think about. What quality of use does the church apply to clergy? to laity and their gifts? to ordained women among the clergy? to those who are handicapped? In what sense does the church's use of human material essentially wound and drain many who would serve it? (an image taken from the parable's incident of beating, killing, and stoning).

He sent his son . . . let us kill him

That same son is the cornerstone of Christian experience. His actual death in history is at the heart of Christian faith. Its consequences are the heart of Christian hope. But in this context we might use the scripture text to examine the place of Our Lord in today's church. In what ways can we, and do we, ''kill'' him in the sense of betraying and diminishing him. When we portray him as the source only of personal grace, we ''kill'' (diminish or ignore) him as the Lord who also demands justice in a society. When we portray him as the giver only of certain gifts (charismatic gifts) and forget the very valid gifts he gives in other ways, we are ''killing'' part of his glory. All of us, even if only by the fact that we cannot completely comprehend Our Lord's glory, become accomplices to his diminishment.

The very stone which the builders rejected has become the head of the corner

It is significant that this statement of Our Lord is in itself a quotation from his own ancient scriptures. Again and again the scriptures sound this theme of the God who works in paradoxes; the God whose ''thoughts are higher than our thoughts and ways higher than our ways''; the God who picks up the piece of material which we have rejected, or who selects the person as his instrument whom we have put aside. Returning to our theme of the church's life, we ask such questions as, What materials are we rejecting which are potentially rich for God's use? What people are we neglecting to call into ministries of many kinds? What gifts are we being blind to?

Psalm

At one level the psalm can be seen as a celebration of Moses' strengths as he begins to end his magnificent ministry of leadership. He has been lawgiver (v 4). He has withstood testing times (v 7). He is the instrument of covenant (vv 9, 10). Now he is free of all that responsibility (v 6). At another level the psalm can be a series of images of the Christian community engaged in a wilderness journey, realizing its dependance on grace (v 7), experiencing some bitter and discouraging times (v 7b), struggling with conflicting and confusing concepts of God (v 9).

Sunday between 9 and 15 October

Deuteronomy 34:1–12
Philippians 4:1–9
Matthew 22:1–14
Psalm 135:1–14

Theme In all three scriptures there is a sense of a point being reached where a future is offered and must be chosen. The Israelites have experienced the death of Moses. A stage is ended in their emergent nationhood (Deuteronomy). In Philippi the church has grown and is cohesive. Now it must choose to consolidate and go ahead (Philippians). In his parable Our Lord shows God as constantly inviting people to enter a kingdom of relationship with God. We must choose to accept the invitation and adapt our lives accordingly (Matthew).

First Reading

There is a deep poignancy about this moment. On the point of death Moses stands on Mount Nebo and sees a panoramic view of the land he has given years of his life to reach.

I have let you see it . . . but you shall not go over there

What is true for Moses at a very high and dramatic level is true in all our lives at an ordinary level.

The simple fact is that there is never a sense of total completion. Our vision of our objectives and hopes always reaches beyond our achievements and contributions. Geoffrey Studdard Kennedy begins one of his poems with the statement, "Lord, there is not one thing done. There is no battle of my life that I have really won." At every stage of our lives — advancing in a career, growing in a relationship, bringing up children — there is a sense of vision and intention always remaining beyond achievement.

The people of Israel wept for Moses . . .
then the days of weeping were ended

There is a healthy ring to that simple statement. It suggests a model for our having to deal with change, endings, stages, partings, death itself. There is no pretending that sorrow doesn't exist, no pretending that something hasn't happened. Rather there is full acknowledgement of reality, and full and fervent expression of our human response to it. But then there comes a time when life must resume, and the journey forward must continue. All of us know the peculiarly tragic situation when someone is not capable of this transition and becomes locked into unending mourning or regret or guilt.

Joshua . . . was full of the Spirit of
wisdom, for Moses had laid his hands on
him

A beautifully balanced statement. The name of Joshua immediately introduces the new age and reality. The name of the future is now Joshua. Yet no sooner is it said than it is linked with a past in the name of Moses. Together both evoke a sense of continuity. In today's church we need to make an effort to point to continuity in the way we study scripture, in our recovery of the long history of spirituality in different ages, in our reaching back to enrich so-called contemporary liturgy. This reaching back is essential as we move into a future of potentially unnerving change. Again we think of the context in which Israel emphasized both past (Moses) and future (Joshua) and linked them to create a sense of continuity. That context was a wilderness. The time we live in is likewise wilderness. Hence the significance of this image of continuity for us.

> *There has not arisen a prophet since in Israel like Moses*

There is here a note that sounds frequently in today's church. It is a feeling that some vague age of great faith or an age of leaders of great stature has passed, that things are not as they were. It is a very human feeling, and whether or not it is ever true (and sometimes it may well be), it is essential that we deal with it sternly and effectively. Israel gave this tribute to Moses, but they worked and built and fought for and supported Joshua. It matters not in the least if the past has in reality been greater in some way. The fact is that it is past. We possess only the present. We are called to serve Our Lord now with the resources among us.

Second Reading   *My brethren whom I love and long for, my joy and crown*

We are at one of the moments when the lyrical and passionate Paul surfaces. This whole reading is beautiful, poetic, and deeply pastoral. In a certain sense it echoes the Deuteronomy passage. Both are an ending or farewell exhortation. Both are also expressions of the deep attachment which forms between any community and the man or woman who has led and cared for that community.

> *I entreat Euodia and Syntyche to agree in the Lord*

Sentiment has not shut off Paul from reality. As always human relationships are less than perfect.

> *Help these women*

Notice how reconciliation is not left to the people themselves. The community is asked to share in the task of reconciling them.

> *Rejoice in the Lord . . . keep your hearts*
> *and minds in Christ Jesus*

These verses might be a portrait of Christian community at its best. Joy, mutual acceptance, a sense of Christ's presence, a lack of anxiety, a rich prayer and intercessary life, a sense of peace. It is a magnificent portrait drawn in swift and vivid strokes.

> *Think about these things. What you*
> *have learned, do*

Notice the balance of reflection and action. Both are necessary if Christian life is to be genuine.

Third Reading   *A king gave a marriage feast*

Once again we have a parable primarily aimed at the situation of Jesus' own time and place. His people have not as a whole responded. Refusing that invitation has a price. Others will be invited.

> *The king . . . sent troops and destroyed*
> *those murderers and burned their city*

It has for long been thought that this is Matthew viewing the Roman destruction of Jerusalem as part of the price paid for rejecting the claims of Our Lord. But having realized the original object of the story, we have to ask how it speaks to us.

Invited to the marriage feast

Immediately we are in a timeless zone. God invites all human life to experience the presence of the divine. For Christians today that invitation can come quite literally as an invitation from a friend. It can be a sudden inexplicable longing to investigate a long-neglected or lost faith. It can be the discovery of the church by one's child and the resulting pressure to respond with the child as parent.

They made light of it and went off

The reasons why the invitation is ignored are in themselves good and valid reasons. In each case other responsibilities come in between guest and acceptance of the invitation. But this is precisely what happens in human experience at such times. The possibility will arise (for the kind of reasons mentioned above) of encountering God and possibly of developing a lasting relationship with the things of Christ and of the Spirit. We are about to accept when perfectly reasonable and worthy things seem to block the way. There is no conscious rejection on our part, merely a choosing of other priorities, or so it seems. We do not intentionally "make light" of God's invitation; we merely give more weight to other things. So we go on intending, when we have time, to worship, to do some Bible study, to learn more about the church, to take more part in its life, to become more invovled in the spiritual quest of our children. On and on our intentions go, but we never actually accept the invitation which sounds deeply inside ourselves. Eventually its sounds grow faint. It moves elsewhere, and others hear and possibly respond.

That whole sequence can also be applied to our relationships. Someone who loves us can be inviting us to the enriching of an actual marriage. Choosing other things, very often job and career, we never consciously refuse the invitation; we merely become otherwise involved. Eventually either the invitation is withdrawn and a relationship dies or, alternatively and as in the parable, the invitation is given to another.

A man who had no wedding garment

When we do accept the invitation of Our Lord, this short additional parable asks a few simple but blunt questions. What is the quality of our acceptance? What investment have we in being his "guest"? What is the depth and reality of our involvement in the Christian community?

Psalm

On one level the psalm can be seen as a song of praise at a certain point in Israel's life. A stage of consolidation is over. Moses' life is ended but they have survived the wilderness. At another level it can be a celebration of such a stage in the life of the Philippi community. God has brought them thus far. The future looks promising. Praise the Lord. But the psalm can also be a song in our own lives. We might pause, reflect on where we are, look back on the way we have got to this point, and try to see where blessing, guidance, and grace were given on the way.

Sunday between 16 and 22 October

Ruth 1:1–19a
1 Thessalonians
1:1–10
Matthew 22:15–22
Psalm 146

Theme Life must be a realistic blending of deep trust in God and wise practical action. We see this mixture in the incidents involving Naomi and Ruth (Ruth). We then see in Thessalonia a community of faith producing an admirable variety of practical actions (Thessalonians). Finally we hear Jesus saying that life must always work out the balance of practical and spiritual in our loyalty to God and to Caesar (Matthew).

First Reading *A certain man of Bethlehem went to sojourn in the land of Moab, he and his wife and his two sons*

Immediately we have a very contemporary image, that of emigration. It may well have been for very contemporary reasons such as job search and economic survival. There is in almost every congregation a family who knows the reality of moving from some "Bethlehem" to some "Moab."

Elimelech, the husband of Naomi, died

Naomi now becomes a familiar contemporary figure, the single parent. Not only that, she must survive without the support systems of her own society. All through our social fabric there are "Naomis," in apartments and condominiums, dealing with some form of "dying," whether it be bereavement itself, or divorce or separation or joblessness.

> *They lived there about ten years; and both [sons] died*

A long time in a life span of those days. That decade could have taken Naomi to the edge of middle age with its further and deeper vulnerabilities. Already she has become the older woman, dependant (in that society) on her sons and their wives. Suddenly disaster strikes, and she finds them also facing widowhood.

> *She started with her daughters-in-law to return from the country of Moab*

The fact that she did so is a grim indication of conditions in Moab. The journey itself would be a major consideration for three woman, even in caravan "protection." We are in fact looking at an image of the still-present vulnerability of singled women in our society. All statistics indicate that the singled woman, either young and with children or elderly and alone, is extremely low on the economic roster. Many are desperate.

> *Return each of you to her mother's house*

The ensuing conversation is about agonizing choices where neither course of action is attractive.

> *Have I yet sons in my womb? I am too*
> *old to have a husband. If I should say I*
> *have hope, even if I should have a*
> *husband this night and should hear sons*

One cannot help but detect a certain agony of longing in the repetitions of Naomi. Her voice is that of many today who in senior years long to be recognized as a sexual person and as one capable of a rich relationship. Her whole speech is a cry against becoming a nonperson in the dance of life.

> *It is exceedingly bitter to me for your*
> *sake that the hand of the Lord has gone*
> *forth against me*

Also present in Naomi is rage, rage against life for what it has done, rage against God. She expresses that rage as we should if we feel it, for its release is very healing.

> *Ruth said, "Entreat me not to leave*
> *you"*

It is one of the great moments of the Bible, and it is expressed with great beauty. It expresses the incalculable value of human relationship, its loyalties and loves. It points to the importance of having at least one strong relationship even if we have nothing else. That in itself can give us the ability to go on as scripture says: "The two of them went on until they came to Bethlehem."

Second Reading   *To the church of the Thessalonians*

As we read Paul corresponding with this long-ago Greek community, we could consider applying his statements to our own Christian community.

*Your work of faith and labour of love and
steadfastness of hope*

We could begin to take these aspects
of that early community and apply them as measuring
criteria for the life of our own church. Using each as a standard, we might ask of our corporate life, Where are there
works of faith? What "labours of love" are being done by
individuals or groups among us? What quality of "hope in
Jesus Christ" do we possess? What can that mean for us?
Perhaps we could ask that same question in this form: How
does our faith in the birth, death, and resurrection of Jesus
Christ affect our attitudes to our world and its events? Does
faith in him give us a basis for hope in the turmoil and
threats of our time?

*Our gospel came to you, in word, in
power, in the Holy Spirit*

Where are such things among us?
What is the quality of "the word" among us? In our corporate life what place and emphasis has scripture? From
the quality of our public lesson reading in worship, to the
formation of Bible study opportunities in our congregation,
what is being done about "the word?" In what sense has
the gospel come among us in power and in the Holy Spirit?
To what extent is our corporate life affecting personal lives,
drawing them to faith and fellowship? If we are using this
particular reading as a homily, it might be immensely effective to ask such questions and have each one responded
to briefly by a man or woman whose experience has been
a response to one or more of these things Paul speaks of.

*You received the word in much affliction,
with joy inspired by the Holy Spirit*

By doing such a homily with a series of very short statements of witness, each one becomes "an example to all the believers."

Third Reading   *To entangle Jesus in his talk*

It may seem a very obvious thing to say, but it is important for us to realize that not everyone who encountered Jesus of Nazareth was attracted to him. There were those who disliked intensely what he said and all he stood for, even to the point of being determined to destroy him. To realize this can help us to come to terms with the fact that not everyone will like us, that there are those, for the most part unknown to us, who heartily dislike us and our attitudes and our efforts, and will probably continue to do so in spite of anything we may try to do about it.

> *You are true . . . [you] teach truthfully . . . [you] care for no man . . . you do not regard the position of men*

Whether or not this was meant sarcastically matters not. The fact that it was said at all indicates what the image of Jesus was among the people. Such attributes are among the most difficult to practice. They add up to a life of complete integrity, unswayed by concerns about personal political survival among the powerful and those able to affect our lives. That integrity is not easy to achieve without considerable courage and risk.

> *Jesus, aware of their malice*

As we see in this short aside about Our Lord, neither he, nor we his followers, have to equate Christianity with naïvety. While we do not have to meet malice with a like enmity, we do need to recognize when and where it exists. Only thus can we challenge it or, if we choose, absorb it without its devastating us. It is much too simple, and it is totally detached from the reality of Jesus, to conceive of him as eternally unresponsive to attack and insult and innuendo.

Render to Caesar . . . and to God

It is, of course, an immortal reply. In a single sentence Jesus delineates the life-long task every man and woman has. He describes the endless choices which must be made. In personal life there are such choices. How do I render God time in a busy life whose every waking moment can become claimed by "Caesar" (the day to day business of life)? The question also comes to many in societies torn by revolution and conflicting loyalties. If I am a socially conscious Christian in an essentially unjust political regime, how do I balance what I render to Caesar and what I render to God. Sometimes men and women work out this complex and dangerous equation at the risk of life itself. Our Lord gives us no neat formula. In his directive lies eternal questions.

Psalm

The psalm is primarily echoing the events of the Ruth passage. It celebrates those who turn to God for help and find their trust vindicated. The admonition to "put not your trust in rulers" does echo Jesus' warning that life is not merely "rendering to Caesar" but also to God. The verses about the Lord caring for the stranger, sustaining the orphan and widow, may well be a valid description of the good work going on in the community at Thessalonica.

Sunday between 23 and 29 October

Ruth 2:1–13
1 Thessalonians 2:1–8
Matthew 22:34–46
Psalm 128

Theme The test of all our pretensions to spirituality is that of loving action. Is it present behind the words and the claims? We see in Boaz the growth of romantic love for Ruth (Ruth). As Paul writes to Thessalonica, he rests the integrity of his ministry on the love ("gentleness and care") which he has shown (1 Thessalonians). To the questioning lawyer Jesus makes it obvious that beyond all claims of law is the ultimacy of love (Matthew).

First Reading

As we read this scripture in the late twentieth century it is salutary to notice how almost every line shows the total dependance on men which dominated a woman's life in that long ago society.

> *Naomi had a kinsman of her husband's,*
> *a man of wealth whose name was Boaz*

Even in death her husband's identity is significant. It is through him and his extended family that there exists a chance of survival. The addition of the phrase "a man of wealth" referring to Boaz is a totally honest acknowledgement that nothing less than survival is at stake for the two women.

> *Ruth said . . . "Let me glean among the ears of corn after him in whose sight I shall find favour"*

The need for survival makes us think clearly and act quickly. Ruth is willing to do the lowest job in the field, mopping up after the reapers. We live in times when many men and women have to do the same. They take any job to survive through a lean time. They take it for exactly the reason Ruth does — so that it may serve as a jumping-off ground to something else.

> *Boaz said . . . "Whose maiden is this?"*

We who know the ending of this story can presume that there are many levels to this moment of encounter. There is, of course, a sexual element present. What takes place is a fascinating and to some extent amusing conversation. It is very typical of the choreography of an initial encounter of the sexes. It has the added ingredient that to Ruth the good graces of this man, even on a level of continued employment, are vital.

> *Do not go to glean in another field. Keep close to my maidens . . . Have I not charged the young men not to molest you?*

Knowingly or not, Boaz sends many signals in this statement. He swiftly claims Ruth as his "territory." A hint of the vulnerability of a solitary foreign woman is given in Boaz's promise of protection in the open field.

*All that you have done for your
mother-in-law*

Boaz's interest is not merely sexual. He
recognizes in Ruth fineness of character.

*You are most gracious to me, my Lord
. . . though I am not one of your
maidservants*

There may well be here both an invita-
tion on Ruth's part to further the relationship, yet at the
same time a hint of determination that she is not prepared
to be merely "one of your (Boaz's) maidservants." The
exchange is all part of the process of this encounter which
will come to mean so much not only for Ruth and Boaz but
also for the future of Israel.

Second Reading   *Our visit to you was not in vain. We
had already suffered . . . at Philippi. We
declared to you the gospel . . . in the
face of great opposition.*

Opposition to Paul in both Philippi
and Thessalonica had been very unpleasant and determined. Yet he had discovered something from the experience. In both communities, as a kind of compensation for
opposition, there had also developed real commitment from
those who did show interest. This experience is an important aspect of today's church life, where issues and communities can so easily suffer great polarization. Trying to
minister across polarized positions may sometimes be
draining and hurtful. Yet sometimes one can discover that,
where there is support, it is as rich in affirmation as opposition is strong in condemnation and hatred. Paul is realizing
this as he writes to Thessalonica. On balance the visit, tough

as it was, has turned out to be worth it. As he says, ''Our visit to you was not in vain.''

> *Our appeal is not made from error or*
> *uncleanness, nor with guile*

Obviously these are all elements in the charges made against Paul by his opposition. But as we read them with ministry today in mind, what might they be saying? They may be good criteria by which we might like to question the integrity of our actions and motivations. ''Error.'' Is it possible that I am mistaken in the position I have taken? Do I need to investigage the situation more than I have? ''Uncleanness.'' What exactly are my motivations for this course of action? Are there reasons for it that I am not prepared to admit are inside me? ''Guile.'' Am I being manipulative of others? What is the relationship between my wish to superimpose my will and my respect for others?

> *We never used words of flattery or a*
> *cloak for greed, nor did we seek glory*
> *from men*

Paul could say that and mean it. Can we? Can we claim that we have never used any such devices to survive or to enhance our activities?

> *We were gentle among you, affectionately*
> *desirous of you, ready to share with you*

In an age like this, a time of anxieties and angers and grimly held attitudes and positions, it is important to see that gentleness need not be weakness, that affection can be felt where there are disagreements, and that sharing can continue in spite of different positions being taken.

> *We were ready to share with you not*
> *only the gospel but also our own selves*

Religion, ministry, church life, even spirituality can be understood and practised in a very cerebral and detached way. We may enjoy sharing official occasions, tasks, interesting ideas and insights and plans. But that is not enough. Christian community asks for the sharing of ourselves. That is less easily done but, when it is, it can be deeply rewarding personally and deeply enriching for the community.

Third Reading   *One of them . . . asked him a question,*
to test him

In our dealings with others it is important to be sensitive to the motivation behind what is said. It is important to discern that, behind a seemingly simple question or statement, there lives something deeper and more significant which the other person may be wishing to hide from us or, quite possibly, communicate to us. Jesus always looked ''through'' statements into the heart of the matter.

> *The great commandment?*

There is, says Jesus, speaking out of the rich insight of his Judaism, only one commandment, only one law — the law to love. We are to love the ultimate reality from whom all things come, and we are to love in the reality in which we are set. Our love for God is tested by the reality of the demands of our neighbour. Biblical religion has no time for a merely disembodied spirituality.

> *What do you think of the Christ?*

The question never ends. It is just as effective and necessary a question for us. How do we make our personal response? Like those who were asked it that day by Jesus himself, we try to define him. They said,

The son of David

Jesus showed the futility of such a definition. Christ could not be that easily defined or, in a sense imprisoned. Jesus' reply really suggests that no neat mental concept does justice to the Christ. This is exactly what we find as we try to wrestle with the meaning of Christ for our day.

Thy enemies under my feet

The ancient gesture of submission to a king. One lay prostrate and his foot was placed on one's neck. The act is mentioned to show that, beyond all efforts to define Christ, to spin any intellectual webs around him, is the necessity to bow to him and to acknowledge him as Lord. Only after that can we begin our search for words to explain, to apply the intellect, to reach definition. As we do so, we are aware that, while there is nothing wrong with our intellectual quest, it will never make Christ its captive.

Psalm

Within these few verses life is quickly and vividly shown at four different levels. First there is the individual in a moment of personal joy. Then there is a glimpse of family life in the home. But in typical biblical fashion personal and family life is placed in the context of society. The first link is the life of the city (Zion). Beyond that is the demand made on all if there is to be a peaceful country and world.

Sunday between 30 October and 5 November

Ruth 4:7–17
*1 Thessalonians
2:9–13, 17–20*
Matthew 23:1–12
Psalm 127

Theme It is a very contemporary theme, that of faith and society. In Ruth's good fortune we see a God who offers to the poor a better future (Ruth). In Paul's words we hear that Christian community is training for life in society (1 Thessalonians). In Our Lord's searing words is a stern criticism of the role of Christian institutions in today's world scene (Matthew).

First Reading

The way this passage begins is the way good homilies should begin. We are immediately presented with a clear and vivid image. This is an exciting moment, and the storyteller is out to make the most of it. Everything that Naomi hardly dared hope for is about to come true!

> *I have bought from the hand of Naomi
> all that belonged to Elimelech and
> Chilion and Mahlon*

This moment is not merely a celebration of a happy ending. We are watching the acting out of a favourite theme of Israel and of the biblical record. It is even more than a favourite theme. It is a passionately held conviction that God is a God who finally vindicates the poor and the helpless and the weak. All of these things Naomi embodies.

> *Also Ruth the Moabitess . . . to be my wife*

The important word in the story is "Moabitess." At certain stages in their history Israel forbade any intermarriage outside its own people. Here we have an inclusive rather than exclusive stance. That is why Ruth's nationality is named once again. Today, both racially and sexually, we are seeking inclusive attitudes in society.

> *May the Lord make this woman . . . like Rachel and Leah*

Such a statement, referring to the very wives of a patriarch of Israel (Jacob), drives home the total acceptance of this "outsider" in Israel.

> *Boaz took Ruth as his wife . . . and she bore a son*

In terms of that society Ruth has achieved the ultimate. From having nothing she has everything. Naomi is not neglected in this joyful episode.

> *Naomi took the child . . . and became his nurse*

The Bible is full of echoes. Another non-Israelite, a princess of Egypt, also handed a child to an older Hebrew woman and asked her to care for it. That child was Moses. The echo in this seemingly casual act is probably deliberate. Ruth's son by Boaz is no ordinary child. He will become the grandfather of David, whose name will shine in Israel's history for ever. For a Christian there is the further significance that one day, far in the future of Ruth and Boaz, a man named Joseph, "of the house and lineage of David," will stand again in Ruth's Bethlehem with his wife Mary, awaiting the birth of their son, Jesus.

Second Reading

This whole passage can be seen as a very beautiful description of the pastoral relationship between priest and people.

We worked night and day

Paul does not mean this literally, nor should it be seen as a literal ideal. To work in that way is not heroic but self-defeating. In the end it is unhelpful to ourselves and to others. But the expression can describe a good attitude to work, one which is generous with its time, which does not watch clocks closely because the task is enjoyed and felt to be an offering.

Our behaviour to you believers

With a priest, as with anyone who claims the privilege of trust and leadership, behaviour and words must be consistent. There will be in him or her mistakes and hurts and many evidences of humanity. But these can and will be forgiven as long as it is seen that there is genuine motivation and integrity.

We exhorted . . . and encouraged you

Paul shows himself to be very wise in this balance. Constant exhortation can become wearying and can provoke resentment. It is essential that encouragement, appreciation, and affirmation are included. Paul himself is sensitive to this.

> *A life worthy of God who calls you into his own kingdom*

One of the most important elements in any pastoral relationship is that men and women hear a call to grow spiritually. Christian faith is not a body of information to be learned nor a destination to be reached. It is an experience in growing in many ways toward becoming the person God is creating.

> *When you received the word of God you accepted it . . . as the word of God*

As a large part of the Christian world chooses a fundamentalist and literal stance to understanding scripture, it is important that other Christian traditions do not merely ridicule that. We need to ask if God is saying something to us through this phenomenon. God may be saying that we ourselves need to recover a sense of the importance of scripture and of the relevance of the Bible to the whole life of the Christian community. There are signs that this is indeed happening. The very fact of new emphases on the Bible in public worship, of more careful standards for those who read it in public worship, of the forming of more Bible study groups and training programs — all these are signs that, while our kind of Christian tradition does not choose a fundamentalist and literal stance to scripture, we are nevertheless reaffirming its high place in the gifts given to us over the centuries.

> *What is our hope or joy or crown of boasting . . . Is it not you?*

We have been looking at this scripture as a portrait of the relationship which can exist between those who minister to a congregation (lay and ordained) and the congregation itself. What is the point of such ministry and its ultimate reward? It is the Christian faith and service which comes about in the lives of those involved in the relationship. The achievement of a priest or lay worker, and the achievement of the congregation as a whole, is the level of ministry released by their relationship.

Third Reading   *They preach but do not practise*

Here is the opposite of what we have been thinking of in the epistle. The test of congregational life is that its "preaching" (its liturgical life) be not just an end in itself but should issue in service. Teaching and practice must exist together if the church's life is to have integrity.

> *They bind heavy burdens . . . on men's shoulders . . . but will not move them*

Sometimes Christian conscience has to recognize that the economic life of a "developed" society places "burdens" (unjust price structures or employment conditions) on others perhaps far away. Christians then have to ask how they themselves can move such burdens.

> *The place of honour at feasts . . . the best seats*

In Western society we have had "the place of honour" at the "feast" of the world's resources. We have, and indeed still have, the "best seat" in the world's standard of living. It is not easy or simple to know what we should do about a privilege which has and does cost other societies dearly. Yet we are called to do so.

Neither be called masters

Our technology, and much else, have made us seem to be masters of the earth, but

He who is greatest . . . shall be your servant

Precisely because we have accumulated power, the question comes as to how we can be of service. How can we serve need?

Whoever exalts himself shall be humbled

We in our society are realizing that, if we exalt ourselves at the cost of others, or at the cost of the environment, we will be humbled. Already in pollution, in acid rain, and in social revolution, we are facing this.

Psalm

The psalm, especially its first half, particularly expresses the applications given above to the Gospel passage. Unless our social fabric (imaged by ''house'' and ''city'') is formed by such biblical principles as justice and mutually concerned relationships, then human activity and all our building of institutions is ''vain.''

All Saints

Revelation 7:9–17
1 John 3:1–3
Matthew 5:1–12
Psalm 34:1–10

Theme Human life and experience are a far more wonderful reality than they appear to be. Viewed with the eyes of faith, they are surrounded by great unseen and often unrealized truths. Any generation or even individual of faith is surrounded by a great host of those who have taken the Christian journey (Revelation). The human search for self-identity culminates in the revelation that we are offspring of God and can choose to grow toward Jesus Christ (John). Finally, surrounding the value systems we take totally for granted, there exists a greater and eternal set of values, those of what Our Lord calls the kingdom of heaven. To the degree that we discover and choose those values we find what he calls "blessedness" or "happiness" (Matthew).

First Reading   *A great multitude . . . from every nation, from all tribes and people*

To a Christian of that early generation, one member of a small minority in a Graeco-Roman city, the concepts of John's vision must have been thrilling. Seen with the eye of faith he or she belonged to a vast company whose bonds stretched beyond time and space into the ultimate reality of God's presence. There are times in personal Christian experience when one feels horribly alone. There are times when a tiny congregation can feel isolated and irrelevant. To such experiences this vision of John can come as inspiration.

Clothed in white robes

For John the white robe suggests that there has been a purifying by suffering. This image can be rich in many ways for reflecting on Christian experience. Much contemporary preaching hesitates to speak of Christian life as a journey toward purification. The ironic fact is that many of the philosophies, cults, and pseudo-religions of our time do not hesitate to do so! We might begin to use the great modern emphasis on physical purifying of our bodies — a balanced and nourishing diet, regular exercise, refraining from smoking. We might seek the spiritual equivalents of such things and reflect on them. What might it mean in Christian terms to seek purification? Do we wish to link that thought with Matthew 5:8 where Our Lord says that the pure in heart are blessed? (We will look at that again in that third reading.)

With palm branches in their hands

When was the last time scripture held this image in front of us? We are standing in the gate at Jerusalem welcoming a rider on a donkey. The fusing of the two images — one very much in time and on earth, the other beyond time and in the heavenly realm — says to us that human experience is lived out against a heavenly background. The small stage on which our actions and decisions are played out is set within a vast stage. An English writer whose many books are based on this conviction is Charles Williams, one of the Inklings Group with C.S. Lewis.

> *The angels . . . the elders . . . the four*
> *living creatures . . . worshipped God*

For us in the late twentieth century the occupants of this cosmic stage can be a reminder of something very contemporary. Notice how the different elements of creation are there — beings above the human, the human itself, the rest of the created life forms. All are worshipping. All respond to the Lord of creation. In all sorts of secular movements modern life is trying to express and live this truth, that our humanity is one with the totality of creation. Here in John's vision we are given magnificent biblical images of it.

> *They fell on their faces and worshipped*
> *God*

Can we imagine the song of all creation? The music of all history, the songs of every generation, the sound of every instrument ever formed by human hand, simple lullabies, great symphonies; with them the music of all the manifestations of nature, thunder, vast rivers, howling wind, trees rustling; the voices of all the animal world, lion's roar, whale song, horse's whinny, dog's bark, the lowing of cattle — all raised and gathered to give glory to their creator. The composer of the Benedicite must have had such a vision in mind many centuries ago.

Second Reading   *See what love the Father has given us*

In these verses of the Epistle John is telling us who we are, and who and what we can become, if we so choose. We are not just bundles of "molecules and atoms" as one of Sean O'Casey's characters loved to say. We are offspring of a creator.

> *We are God's children now; it does not yet appear what we shall be, but . . . we shall be like him*

In one sense the future is hidden from us. We do not know what we shall become. Yet we do know what we may become if we choose to become aware of the face of reality which we see in Jesus Christ. Our becoming can be in that pattern. He can be the model for our conscious formation.

When he appears

It would be wrong to attach Our Lord's appearance to some far distant moment at the end of time. Christian living is carried out in the conviction that Our Lord constantly appears, in fact that there is no part of our daily experience in which Our Lord is not somewhere appearing! That appearing is always in disguise. Only in the unreality of cheap media images of religion are there shining lights and unseen voices and celestial choirs! There is an ironic meaning to John's words that follow below.

When he appears we shall be like him

We might use this phrase to remind ourselves that, when Our Lord appears, he is among us and for us, as someone like us and we like him! Our friend in need is like Jesus precisely because Jesus is in him or her. The voice of a friend — a voice just like ours, telling us lovingly something about ourselves that we don't want to hear — can be the voice of Jesus. The claim of Christian faith is not merely that Our Lord will appear but that he is always appearing.

> *Every one who thus hopes in him purifies himself as he is pure*

To possess Jesus Christ as a reality in our lives, as a focus for our living, as a central point of meaning and reference, is to possess a basis for hope in our lives. To possess such a basis for hope can "purify" our lives of such shadowed things as hopelessness, anxiety, fear, alienation — to mention only a few. Impurity has become understood in such a limited way in our culture that it now has little more than vague sexual connotations, thought by many to be dated and almost irrelevant! To understand human life as pure is much deeper and all embracing. It means getting our lives together as a whole, and for a Christian the pattern of that wholeness is nothing less than the life of Jesus Christ as Lord. We purify ourselves "as he is pure."

Third Reading   *Seeing the crowds he went up on the mountain*

The scene is a mirror image of the dream of John in Revelation. Once more there is the central figure surrounded by crowds. As Matthew writes this passage, there is yet another mirror image in his mind, that of Moses on Mount Sinai bringing God's law to Israel.

> *His disciples came to him*

It may seem a very obvious thing to say, but this statement is not merely about a past event.

This gathering of disciples is acted out again and again when and wherever Christians gather. When we meet for Bible study, we are gathering around Christ as the Word. When we meet for eucharist, we gather around Christ as bread and wine. When we meet for the sacrament of baptism, we gather around Christ as living water.

Blessed are the poor in spirit

To realize that we have spiritual needs is to open the way for them to flow toward us. The real tragedy is when there exists no such sense of need. There is then no sense of searching, no sense of spiritual journey. One is under the pitiable illusion that one has already entered the kingdom of heaven, thus ironically ensuring that one never will!

Blessed are those who mourn for they shall be comforted

Our Lord's insight anticipates those insights we have gained psychologically in this century. We know all too well that, unless we indeed mourn, unless we fully acknowledge our loss, we cannot receive any resources offered to comfort us.

Blessed are the meek, for they shall inherit the earth

More than any other sentence this particular remark of Our Lord shows exactly his intention in the Beatitudes. This statement flies in the teeth of all human experience in society. Every element of our professional lives contradicts and is contradicted by this statement of Jesus. As we listen to it, we could be tempted almost to pity its seeming naivety. Yet when we remind ourselves of its source — the lips of Our Lord himself — we are brought up sharply. We are forced to acknowledge that at this point, as at many others, the categories of the kingdom of God turn the taken-for-granted categories of this world upside down.

> *Blessed are those who hunger and thirst for righteousness, for they shall be satisfied*

I find the expression of this beatitude in the New English Bible very helpful. It refers to those "who hunger and thirst to see right prevail." Our Lord is not saying that such a deeply committed person is necessarily going to have their constant quest for justice and the right and the good satisfied. Obviously that cannot be true. What he is saying is that such a quest in life, though it will often know frustration and disappointment, gives a person deep satisfaction.

> *Blessed are the merciful for they shall obtain mercy*

Particularly in professional life, and even more if we rise to an executive level, we often have choices about how we deal with others. It may be those within the organization. It may be those very distant from us, who nevertheless may be affected by decisions of investment or corporate policy. Probably as good a definition as any for the phrase "having mercy" would be taking all the elements of a situation into account, especially the human factors.

> *Blessed are the pure in heart for they shall see God*

What might it mean to be pure in heart? Surely sincerity must be included. Might it also mean that the motivations for our actions are not mixed with any sense of meanness, self-advantage, or betrayal? When Our Lord says that such a life can bring us to "see God," he is suggesting that to hold such single-mindedness is to see life as God sees it, to be for others, to long for the welfare of others.

> *Blessed are the peace makers for they*
> *shall be called the sons of God*

The emphasis is on the "makers" of peace. More and more in our own time we are realizing that peace is not merely a blissful state to be envisioned and awaited. Instead we are realizing that peace is a reality which needs the same level of planning, thought, action, and sacrifice as any other end we desire. It is easy to miss the immense emphasis Our Lord places on this particular activity. Even within the life of the church those who give their energies to peacemaking find themselves receiving such names as "left wing," "radical," "subversive." Here we find Our Lord giving such men and women the highest of titles.

> *Blessed are those who are persecuted for*
> *righteousness' sake*

Our Lord is saying that the highest human activity is to seek justice and the right of others, even when it entails great cost to oneself.

> *Blessed are you when men revile you*
> *. . . on my account*

Christian faith as something costly, demanding courage and sacrifice, is unfamiliar to most North American Christians but not, of course, entirely absent from the experience of many. The courage to question public policy or corporate decisions from within an organization, the courage to challenge emerging trends in such things as the commercial use of Sunday, can be costly and can make one the object of ridicule and enmity. Elsewhere in the world there are steadily increasing circumstances where Christian faith can become the focus of intense hatred.

Psalm

A vividly drawn portrait of the totally God-centred life. The first three verses express an attitude of constant praise. Then there is the acknowledgement of God as support where we are most deeply vulnerable (vv 4, 6,7). God is the source of human joy (vv 5, 8). A final burst of affirmation names God as the source of all worth and meaning in human experience (vv 9, 10). Such a centred life is what sainthood really means.

Sunday between 6 and 12 November

Amos 5:18–24
1 Thessalonians
4:13–18
Matthew 25:1–13
Psalm 50:7–15

Theme Our humanity is created for, and called to encounter with, God. We experience that encounter in many ways. Amos shows us that our efforts to encounter God are of no avail if there is not a corresponding living out of justice and integrity (Amos). Paul tells us that the whole human race, through the mystery of resurrection, is destined for encounter with God (1 Thessalonians). In Our Lord's parable we learn that encounter with God can demand a lasting and resilient faithfulness (Matthew).

First Reading

Woe to you who desire the day of the Lord

In every society there is a great deal of sentimental religion. It assumes a gentle avuncular god who comforts and guides, sends guardian angels, and can listen for ever to sweet music about Jesus! This god is essentially accepting of whatever way of life we lead because he is full of love and forgiveness. If we do step out of line now and again, god is a reasonable person who can wink a blind eye. Above all, this kind of god sticks to religion and is not involved in the harsher realities of life. It is at something like this that Amos is lashing out. He would have called such a concept of God an idol!

> *Why would you have the day of the*
> *Lord? It is darkness and not light*

We have a phrase in English which says that something "is not all sweetness and light." There is, cries out Amos, a whole other side to the reality we so glibly call God, and that side is nothing short of terrifying. To encounter that God is not to encounter darkness in the sense of evil but in the sense of deep and terrible mystery.

> *As if a man fled from a lion and a bear*
> *met him . . . leaned his hand against a*
> *wall and a serpent bit him*

Sometimes, Amos is saying, to encounter a God who demands accountability is to get a terrible surprise. Where we expect support and approval for our actions and policies, we receive sudden and painful correction.

> *I despise your feasts*

Religion which is mere ritual without real commitment to that which the ritual expresses is contemptible. One by one Amos denounces the symbols of the ritual of his day, exposing the moral vacuum beneath them. Perhaps it is important to say that neither Amos nor any other prophet decries the loveliness and dignity of liturgical action and music and language. It is only when there exist no corresponding moral realities in the worshipper or in the society that Amos and others feel driven to question and challenge religious activity.

*Let justice roll down like waters, and
righteousness like an everflowing stream*

Amos was not a mere faultfinder,
eloquently expressing what he didn't want! Here, in one
of the most ringing and memorable statements in scripture,
he expresses the great moral imperatives of justice and
righteousness. That demand has always been an element
of both Judaism and Christianity. Frequently it has lan-
guished, becoming the forlorn quest of small minorities. In
the late twentieth century that quest has become the intense
commitment of multitudes of Christians who have come to
see in the eucharist the pattern and vision of a community
of justice and acceptance and equality.

Second Reading   *That you may not grieve as others do
who have no hope*

While Paul is responding to early
Christian concerns about those who have died before the
return of the Lord, the words speak to any Christian in any
age. In our living of life and our facing the inevitability of
death, there is no escape from grieving, whether for
ourselves or for another. For many reasons we tend to
neglect either Bible study or preaching on such themes as
dying, death, and the after-life. We tend to deal with these
things only when death is present. Yet modern minds need
to recapture those scriptural sources on which Christian
hope beyond death is based. This is even more necessary
in a society which is doubtful about the future of the race
itself and therefore is bereft of a hope even within history.

We believe that Jesus died and rose again

Those eight words are the central ci-
tadel of Christian faith. They are the expression of the
timeless hope that Christian faith offers to our human condition in the face of death.

*We who are alive, who are left until the
coming of the Lord*

All Christians in any age live between
the life of Jesus and the coming of Christ. That means that
a Christian lives in a time and a history which has meaning and purpose under the rule of God. Within that time,
however long it may be, a Christian regards his or her life
as finally accountable to the Lord of history, by whose will
time and creation fulfil his purpose.

*The Lord will descend from heaven with
a cry of command, with the archangel's
call, with the sound of the trumpet*

Such were the natural images for Paul
to use in his tradition. We may reach for other images by
which to try to express what the final claiming of history
and creation may be like. Whatever images we use, they
will seek to express a single truth. That truth is in the images
Paul uses. All his images emphasize the majestic authority
of God.

*The dead in Christ will rise first . . .
then we who are alive shall be caught up
to meet the Lord in the air*

Paul paints a haunting picture of the
human race drawn inexorably to a rendezvous with God.
That is the essential truth being conveyed. In other images
Pierre Teilhard de Chardin spoke of this as our human
destiny. The great realities we have heard Paul express,
realities for which every culture and every age strives to find
adequate description, have not changed one iota. The first
is that the will and purpose of God is the ultimate authority for creation, its beginning and end. The second is that

human nature, the totality of human nature embodied through time in succeeding mortal generations, is the creation of God and will be called to ultimate account by God.

Third Reading   *Ten maidens took their lamps . . . five of them were foolish, and five were wise*

In relation to Jesus' vision of the kingdom, what are foolishness and wisdom? They seem to be two different qualities in our spirituality which are often mentioned in scripture.

The bridegroom was delayed

One quality is our ability to live out a sustained, lasting faith. Such a faith is different from the sudden burst of ecstatic spirituality. It endures through thick and thin. It is a "for better or for worse" faith. It is very aware that the kingdom of God does not come overnight into human lives or relationships or societies. In terms of this parable, it is a faith which has enough oil in its lamp to keep the flame alight.

Behold the bridegroom

The other quality is that of living in constant expectation of the approach of God. It is to live each day, to enter into every experience and situation, with the anticipation that God may use this particular place or time or circumstance to encounter us. No warning will be given. No guarantees that God will or will not be present. Suddenly we will be aware of that presence.

Give us some of your oil

The request is met by a refusal. The reason given is that there will not be enough for two sets of lamps. In terms of faith, however, the real reason why the request must be refused is that faith must always be a personally fostered possession. The resources to keep its flame alight must come from a personal commitment. Faith can be caught from someone else. It can be fanned into flame in us by someone else's love or encouragement or sacrifice, but once ignited, our own commitment must go to keeping it alight.

Psalm

The verses primarily echo the theme of the first reading. They express the new insights about the nature of God which Israel is moving toward. It is not a dismissal of their worship of sacrifices but a recognition that that is not enough. What must be offered to God is the heart, the whole self. There is an echo of the Gospel in the opening verse. Salvation will be shown for those who keep in the way — whose faith is lasting and resilient.

Sunday between 13 and 19 November

Zephaniah 1:7,12–18
1 Thessalonians
5:1–11
Matthew 25:14–30
Psalm 76

Theme All three readings are linked by images of our being accountable before God. We are shown a grim portrait of divine judgement on the human story (Zephaniah). Paul points to the choices we must make in response to our time and our society (1 Thessalonians). Finally Our Lord makes it very clear that we can choose our response to being accountable. We can refuse life or we can celebrate and develop it (Matthew).

First Reading

We are listening to the voice of a man living in a society which has barely survived nearly half a century of appallingly corrupt rule. The name of the ruler, now only a few years dead, was Manasseh. We hear the voice of Zephaniah much as we might have heard the dire predictions of someone who had lived through the disintegration of Ugandan life and instutions under Idi Amin in this century.

The day of the Lord is at hand

The time has come when the consequences of past actions and policies must be faced. In many ways our own age is such a time. When we say that we must face the consequences of such things as careless land and resource use or economic exploitation of certain societies, we are saying that "the day of the Lord is at hand." When Zephaniah uses language such as

> *The Lord has prepared a sacrifice*

He may be saying what we today might express in this way — "God as the Lord of history is presenting us with the bill for our actions." When Zephaniah speaks about those

> *Who say in their hearts, "The Lord will not do good, nor will he do ill"*

The prophet is referring to an attitude very prevalent in our secularized Western society. Millions among us would rephrase Zephaniah's statement by saying that God is irrelevant to contemporary decision making.

> *Their goods shall be plundered, their houses laid waste . . . the mighty man cries aloud there*

If the day of the Lord is understood as retribution and the consequence of history, then we are living at such a time. By revolutionary change and seemingly irrational violence, many "goods are plundered" and "houses laid waste" and "the mighty man" is made to cry aloud for past policies and actions.

> *A day of distress and anguish, of ruin and devastation . . . of battle cry against fortified cities and against lofty battlements*

Zephaniah heaps condemnation upon the all too prevalent militarism of his day. He is thinking of fortified cities both within his own small country and in Egypt and Assyria. He warns that "their silver and their gold" will not be able to deliver them; after continued power struggle even the best economy eventually collapses. In no way does Zephaniah take sides. It is not for him a scenario of "good guys" and "bad guys." Judgement on a way of life, on the impulses and enmities which are motivating all societies, is Zephaniah's message. For him there is the possibility of "sudden end . . . of all the inhabitants of the earth." In our own age it is being recognized that such "a sudden end . . . of all the inhabitants of the earth" is quite possible. As we contemplate that possibility we realize more and more that "the day of the Lord" is not the action of a vengeful and wrathful God but the consequences of human choices and actions. We can bring upon ourselves "the day of the Lord," for it is our tragedy and our glory that we are creatures both flawed and free. In that freedom, of course, lies hope.

Second Reading   *The day of the Lord will come like a thief in the night*

A statement true on many levels. Paul is saying that God's calling the human race to an accounting will be sudden, without warning. This truth is experienced in many senses. A course of conduct will be pursued with seeming success for some time. Suddenly there are consequences. A marriage will continue in spite of certain strains until suddenly a crisis comes. In the experience of Western technical advancement, there seemed no end to achievement. Suddenly we face the possibility of self-extinction.

You are not in darkness . . . we are not of the night

Paul is simply saying that being a
Christian gives one an awareness that all human existence
is accountable, always and at any moment accountable.

> *Let us not sleep, as others do . . . let us*
> *keep awake and be sober*

Paul is talking about the attitudes and
lifestyles we choose in the time we are asked to live in. Do
we hide from the realities of our time (i.e. "sleep"), or do
we face those realities while doing our best to respond to
them creatively and constructively.

> *Those who sleep . . . those who get*
> *drunk*

Paul is describing a situation we see
in our own time. If we think of "sleep" and "get drunk"
as images of something widespread, then we recognize a
contemporary pattern. That "something" is the tendancy
in a very demanding age to deal with life either by retreat
and opting out ("sleep"), or by indulgence in appetite and
over-consumption of some kind.

> *Let us put on the breastplate of faith and*
> *love, . . . the hope of salvation*

Faith, hope, and love are Paul's
great trio, mentioned again and again. They are the oppo-
sites of despair, hopelessness, and alienation — all so much
part of life in his age and in ours. What for Paul is the basis
of faith, hope, and love? What makes it possible to choose
such values in such an age? His conviction is that the Christ
has made possible a new understanding of our human condition, if we choose to apply his sacrifice and his triumph
to our own living.

Third Reading   *Entrusted to them his property*

Everything we have and are is in the first place God's. If that sounds obvious, it is frequently forgotten. One cannot as a Christian boast of one's gifts. One can merely give thanks for them because that is precisely what they are — gifts of God.

> *To one . . . five talents to another two . . . to another one*

Our Lord's portrait of human life is certainly not egalitarian! We are given different and not necessarily equal gifts. But the phrase ''each according to his ability'' is significant. Each is asked to use his own gifts. The recipients are not in competition with each other. They are asked only to celebrate and to develop their gifts. To view one's own life in this way is to enhance the possibility of a balanced and fulfilled life.

> *I have made five talents more . . . I have made two talents more*

Each claims to have developed the gifts given to him. Each is asked to enter into the master's joy. The parable perhaps implies that to develop one's gifts is to discover the sheer joy of living.

> *I went and hid your talent in the ground*

Notice what assumptions precede this. His view of God (of reality?) is such that life is not thought of in terms of celebration and affirmation. Life is guilt ridden, motivated by fear. The relationship between our humanity and God is adversarial, mistrustful, sad. If so, our instinctive response is to bear a poor self-image, to mistrust our own abilities. To use the monetary image of talents, we "short change" ourselves. To use the image of the man digging, we "dig in" or "we bury" our abilities.

> *Here you have what is yours*

We do not destroy our abilities, but by our defensiveness and fear we ensure that they never grow. By doing this we discover too late a terrible truth.

> *You ought to have invested . . . To everyone who has will more be given. From him who has not, even what he has will be taken*

We discover that to hoard a gift is to ensure that it will shrivel up. As Jesus says elsewhere, there is a terrible contradiction deep in life by which we discover that the more we try to save life in the wrong sense the more certain we are to lose it. The result is lifelong regret.

Psalm
Like a chorus the word *judgement* sounds again and again. But God's judgement is never a mere condemnation of human life. It is always a moral judgement. It makes a moral demand, especially when it refers to "the oppressed of the earth." God is also portrayed as the one to whom we bring our human gifts.

Last Sunday after Pentecost:
The Reign of Christ

Ezekiel 34:11–16,
20-24
1 Corinthians
15:20–28
Matthew 25:31–46
Psalm 23

Theme Each of the scriptures gives us a set of images of sovereignty. That sovereignty or "reign" is first seen in terms of the pastoral relationship between God and his people (Ezekiel). By entering our humanity God in Christ shows our humanity capable of reigning even over death (1 Corinthians). In the panorama of cosmic judgement we see acts of caring and love reigning above all other criteria as humanity is called to account (Matthew).

First Reading

Thus says the Lord God . . . I myself
will search for my sheep

The familiarity of this statement can blind us to its wonder. It is easy to forget the depth of insight and the spiritual journeying that led Israel to realize that the creator of the universe is concerned about humanity. The fact inspires awe. The word they so often used for it is *covenant*. The reason why it is so important for us to grasp the great fact of humanity and God being in a covenanted relationship is that millions of people no longer believe this, or at least find it extremely difficult to believe.

> *I will rescue them from all places where*
> *they have been scattered . . . I will bring*
> *them out from the peoples*

We can recognize the power of this passage for a Jewish reader. For him or her it has a primary meaning that points to the land of Israel. For a Christian reader this passage might suggest a pattern for the work of the church in the late twentieth century. Increasingly we see church life as having to serve people scattered throughout a culture, mingling with many others who do not share Christian faith, who may even have contempt for faith as such. Many modern congregations are scattered across great cities. Most Christians function from Monday to Friday in situations which in no way reflect the affirmations and ideals expressed in worship.

> *I will feed them on the mountains of*
> *Israel*

If we think of the church building as a "high place" in the ancient sense, a place where men and women reach for the heights within themselves and toward the presence and grace of God, then the church exists to feed the people of God, whether it be a eucharistic feeding, a feeding of the mind in study, or a feeding of the soul in devotional practice. That feeding is not merely from some official church existing above and apart from its people. Rather, the feeding in a Christian community is mutual, made possible by a constant sharing of the gifts of each one.

> *I will feed them with good pasture . . .*
> *in good grazing land . . . on fat pasture*

The emphasis is on quality. This is precisely what God is demanding of contemporary church life, that it be of the finest quality. Worship, Bible study, prayer life, outreach into the society — all must be well done because the challenge to Christian faith and practice can be so all-pervading and strong.

> *I myself will be the shepherd of my sheep*

As a Christian reads this, he or she must be conscious of the thrilling secret or hint about the still unknown future. God will indeed, in Christ, become shepherd to his people.

> *I will seek the lost . . . strengthen the weak . . . the fat and the strong I will watch over . . . I will feed them in justice*

There in a set of images is the gentle and yet stern nature of God. Those images are also the charter of the church, one which is being demanded with a fearful urgency in our age. The call for pastoral faithfulness goes side by side with the call for justice to be sought and to be done. There is an even more chilling indication in that the words "watch over" are in some manuscripts rendered as "destroy."

Second Reading *In fact, Christ has been raised from the dead*

Here is the heart of the Christian good news. In so far as we are celebrating the "reign of Christ" today, then it is in this fact that Our Lord supremely reigns.

> *The first fruits of those who have fallen asleep*

Paul is saying that Our Lord's victory is not an isolated event. It is linked to our human experience.

> *By man (humanity) came death by man came also the resurrection of the dead*

The hope and glory of humanity is that it has been taken and glorified by Our Lord's entering it and taking it on himself. It is not a case of humanity being the means of entry to the world and death, and divinity being the means of life. Both exist now in the same humanity which holds the choice of the entry of death or life into the world in a most literal and technical sense.

> *Then comes the end . . . He must reign until he has put all enemies under his feet*

Paul is stretching his own mind here to the utmost as he tries to communicate a vision. It is a vision of a universe no longer in moral struggle but totally under the dominion of God. It is the same vision as that which Isaiah tries to express. It is the vision of Our Lord when he speaks the parables of the "kingdom." It is also the vision of John of Patmos, seen in terms of the Holy City. What Paul is expressing is so vast that language and thought and imagination fail when we grapple with the vision. Yet even though we cannot fully articulate that vision, it is deep in human consciousness. The conviction that creation will find fulfilment and final purpose is to a great extent the fuel and inspiration for all human thought and activity, even when we fail to acknowledge the existence of such a conviction.

Third Reading   *When the Son of man comes in his glory*

There is a kind of vast "operatic" quality about these opening verses. A cosmic stage is set. Time and history and all humanity are contained within it.

> *He will separate . . . the sheep at his right hand the goats at the left*

Notice the complete absence of any elements of our familiar Western courtroom arguing before the judge! The verdict is long in! The accumulated policies and decisions, presumably taken on the basis of the age-old justification we call national self-interest, are now being judged and evaluated. All the personal decisions and actions and motivations of human lives have formed creatures capable or incapable of being servants of the Son of man.

> *Come . . . inherit the kingdom. Depart . . . into the eternal fire*

The gulf between the two is ultimate. It would seem, however, that there is a hint about God's selection criteria. It seems to be on the basis of there being some who can grow more, who can responsibly continue their present journey; for surely entry into a kingdom means to travel further spiritually.

> *Hungry, you gave me food . . . thirsty, you gave me drink . . . a stranger, you welcomed me*

It is when we look to see what the categories of spirituality are that we can be surprised. In a way the categories are so unspiritual, at least by some views of what is "spiritual." There are Christians who dismiss such activities as "mere social action," as "humanist." Yet here we see them elevated to the highest priority. They are shown to be the basis on which the whole of human life is judged.

Many Christians take no issue with feeding the hungry, welcoming the stranger, visiting the prisoner, as long as these activities are carried out on an individual and apolitical basis. What sometimes causes alarm is when the activities of the Christian community go deeper than mere personal charity, when they probe into the causes which bring about human suffering. Helder Camara, archbishop of Recife in Brazil has put it succinctly: "When I gave the poor bread, they called me a saint. When I asked why the poor were hungry they called me a Marxist." Because it forces us to think in terms deeper than that of individual need and individual suffering, this passage is extremely powerful.

Psalm

This psalm must surely be among those things which we suspect will last as long as the human story continues. It remains deeply personal all through and so seems to echo the Ezekiel passage clearly. God is a God who cares for his people. Yet, in so far as that same caring is demanded of God's people (Christians being Christ's body in the world), the psalm echoes the call for caring and justice in Matthew's passage.